HUNDRED
PERCENTERS

HUNDRED
PERCENTERS

CHALLENGE YOUR EMPLOYEES TO GIVE IT THEIR ALL, AND THEY'LL GIVE YOU EVEN MORE

MARK MURPHY

New York   Chicago   San Francisco   Lisbon   London   Madrid   Mexico City
Milan   New Delhi   San Juan   Seoul   Singapore   Sydney   Toronto

The *McGraw·Hill* Companies

3 4 5 6 7 8 9 0   DOC/DOC   0 1 0

ISBN 978-0-07-163894-4
MHID 0-07-163894-6

McGraw-Hill books are available at special quantity discounts to use as premiums and sales promotions, or for use in corporate training programs. To contact a representative, please e-mail us at bulksales@mcgraw-hill.com.

This book is printed on acid-free paper.

Library of Congress Cataloging-in-Publication Data
Murphy, Mark A. (Mark Andrew)
    Hundred percenters : challenge your employees to give it their all, and they'll give you even more / by Mark Murphy
        p. cm.
    ISBN 978-0-07-163894-4 (alk. paper)
1. Employee motivation.   2. Achievement motivation   3. Goal setting in personnel management.   4. Supervision of employees.   I. Title.

    HF5549.5.M63M867 2010
    658.3'14—dc22

                                                        2009025984

To Andrea, Isabella, and Andrew

Contents

Acknowledgments

I hate to be cliché, but there really are too many people to thank individually for making contributions to this book. My team of several dozen researchers and trainers, and each of our hundreds of fantastic clients, deserve a special thank you. This book, and the research behind it, wouldn't exist without all their efforts.

I would also like to highlight three individuals who made special contributions to this particular book.

Andrea Burgio-Murphy, Ph.D., is a world-class clinical psychologist, my wife and partner through life, and my creative sounding board. Since we started dating in high school, I have learned something from her every single day. My personal and professional evolution owes everything to her.

Lyn Adler is an exceptional writer who has worked with me for several years. Lyn's assistance made it possible to distill mountains of research and interviews into this contribution to the leadership literature.

Mary Glenn, editorial director at McGraw-Hill, deserves a very special thank you for recognizing the need for this book and making the process fast and smooth. After working with Mary and the team at McGraw-Hill, it's very clear to me why the best business thinkers sign with them.

Introduction

Peek out your office door and take a good look at your employees. With the exception of a few royal pains, you've got a nice group of people. By and large, they do good work, they get along with you and one another, and they're generally well intentioned. Given all that, it would only be natural if you felt pretty satisfied with your team and your leadership.

But now look a little harder. Are they giving 100%? Are they pushing themselves to their limits and beyond? Right now, are they dripping blood, sweat, and tears to achieve greatness? When they leave today, will they be giving that Tiger Woods fist pump, chanting to themselves, "Damn, we're good! That was hard work, but we came through like champs." Or will they be dully muttering, "Another day, another dollar"?

If Leadership IQ's research on more than 500,000 employees and leaders is any indication, out your door you see a lot more "OKness" than "greatness." You probably see a lot more "getting by" and "pretty satisfied" than you see "I want to taste victory at the top of the mountain no matter how steep the climb."

Right now, 77% of leaders believe their employees are not giving 100%. And they're not far off in their assessment, because 72% of employees admit they're not giving 100%. Plenty of people are doing fine work, getting by, and delivering products and services to customers. But disappointingly small minorities are coming in every day saying, "Let's push the envelope, let's be great, let's do what nobody thought could be done, let's not have satisfied customers—instead let's have evangelists—and let's feel that deep fulfillment and pride that only comes from hard-won victory."

You might be frustrated that not everyone is a Hundred Percenter (the people who give 100%). Maybe you're irritated that we seem to be falling so short of our potential. Maybe you look at the Wall Street collapse and ask, "Why didn't we push ourselves to understand, and acknowledge, the full extent of the risks inherent in these complex derivatives?" Maybe you look at our Big Three automakers and ask, "How did we get this complacent and out of touch in the face of such intense competition?" Maybe you look at our educational system and ask, "How can the richest country on earth rank twenty-third in the world in math skills?" Maybe you look at our health-care system and ask, "How can the country with the Mayo Clinic and Johns Hopkins rank forty-fifth in the world in infant mortality?"

Outside of work, maybe you're irritated that the service you get isn't that great, or that products don't seem to last very long, or that the person who just took your order literally rolled his eyes when you substituted mashed potatoes for fries. At work, maybe you're wondering what you need to put in your water to make people tap their creative potential like they do at Google, throw design limitations out the window like they do at Apple, give 100% service like they do at the Ritz-Carlton, or push the envelope on efficiency like they do at Toyota.

Maybe you're a bit peeved because you know that we've given 100% before. Compare us with the members of the Greatest Generation, who won World War II, conquered tyranny, ended the

Great Depression, rebuilt the country, all while sacrificing economically and burying over 400,000 of their sons and daughters (and please remember that our population at the time was half of what it is currently, so that number would really be more like 800,000 today). Were they sitting around saying, "Well, I guess as long as I'm fairly content, everything will be okay, so there's no need to really push myself"? Or did they aspire to something extraordinary, purposefully and indefatigably storm through every obstacle to achieve it, and then live their lives with a confidence and pride known only to other Hundred Percenters?

This book will show you how to be the kind of leader that creates Hundred Percenters. It's for everyone who believes that Hundred Percenters get better results, feel more deeply fulfilled, and are the key to every great corporate and cultural achievement. This book is for every leader who believes that people have more potential than they're presently using—that everyone can be a Hundred Percenter. That the iPod, the X-Box, the Amazon Kindle, Google, the Human Genome Project, etc., were created by Hundred Percenters. That Hundred Percenters won World War II, won the cold war, put a man on the moon, created the polio vaccine, and are the key to our future success. That if we care enough to push ourselves and one another past our self-imposed limitations, past the lure of being good enough, we will achieve results even dreamers haven't yet envisioned.

The 100% Leader

The 100% Leader creates Hundred Percenters. The 100% Leader takes average people, and by challenging them and creating a connection with them, unleashes their true potential to achieve extraordinary results. The 100% Leader doesn't just accept people as they are; the 100% Leader sees what we could become and cares enough to push us beyond self-imposed limitations to realize that potential.

Since I founded Leadership IQ, we have studied more than 125,000 leaders. We've analyzed their styles, decisions, and actions and the hard and soft outcomes that result. We wanted to know which leaders generated the most profits, had the greatest innovations, achieved the highest productivity, and had the lowest turnover, among other indicators. After all the regressions, factor analyses, and just plain common sense, we discovered that the two most important differentiating factors in separating exceptional from average leaders are Challenge and Connection.

Connection is the strength of the emotional connection a leader builds with his or her people—do employees share openly, do they want the leader's feedback (positive or constructive), do they believe the leader really cares about their success, and do they trust the leader's intentions?

Challenge is the extent to which a leader pushes his or her folks—how difficult are the assignments, how much do they make people stretch, and do people ask to develop skills in areas where they haven't yet developed an obvious aptitude?

Two of the most important decisions you have to make as a leader are how much you want to challenge your folks to push their limits and how tight an emotional bond you want to build with them. The decisions you make on these two issues will determine exactly what kind of leader you're going to be.

After analyzing leaders' performance on these two dimensions, we've been able to "type" the four major styles of leaders, as shown in Figure I-1.

As you can see from the figure, if you don't challenge people and you don't build an emotional bond with them, you're an Avoider (you're also not doing much that could be called leading). If you challenge people to exceed their limits but you don't have

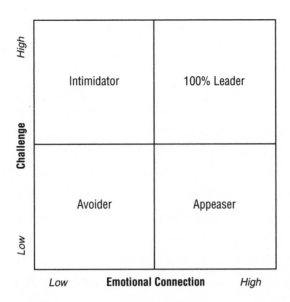

Figure I-1

much of a connection with them, you're an Intimidator. If you connect with your folks but you don't challenge them all that much, you're an Appeaser. And if you issue great challenges while still building intense connections with people, you're the ultradesirable 100% Leader. (You can take a test on www.leadershipiq.com to see where you fall.)

Now, it's nice to know what style you are, but which style is ultimately the most effective? (After all, if being a jerk got better results, who could argue with being a jerk?) Here's where our 360° leadership evaluations become extremely useful. If you're not familiar with the tool, a 360° assessment is when a leader is evaluated by bosses, colleagues, employees, and even customers. It's like a 360° walk around a leader to see his or her performance from everyone's perspective.

Let's look at one of our recent studies. We selected a pool of roughly 17,000 leaders for whom we had data on 360° assessments, budget performance (whether cost or profit centers), employee turnover, employee surveys, and, for a smaller subset, a measure of innovativeness. We then selected the top 10% of performers on budget, turnover, and innovativeness to see what kinds of leadership assessments they received. (*Full disclosure:* While we have very robust rules to ensure the objectivity of our research, these leaders were drawn from paying clients who engaged us to assess and improve their leaders.)

The top 10% of budget performers were those who either made the most profit or came in most under budget (in coordination with the respective client organizations, we made every attempt to weed out those who dangerously slashed budgets and, in the process, did serious damage to their departments). What we found was that, overwhelmingly, the best performers were 100% Leaders. Looking at Figure I-2, you'll see that some leaned toward Intimidators, as Challenge seemed slightly more important than Connection here, but the numbers weren't significant.

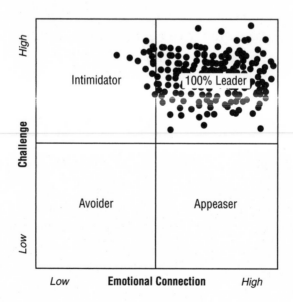

Figure I-2

The top 10% of employee turnover performers were those who had the lowest voluntary turnover (essentially, employees who left on their own without being terminated). Again, what we found was that, overwhelmingly, the best performers were 100% Leaders. This time, as you can see in Figure I-3, there were some who leaned toward Appeasers, as Connection was slightly more important than Challenge, but not in significant numbers.

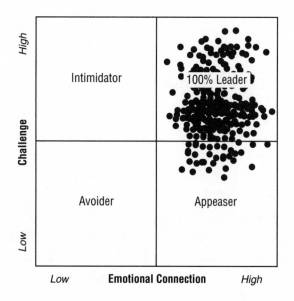

Figure I-3

And the top 10% of performers on innovativeness were determined by the senior leaders at each client organization (they could assess product innovations, service innovations, efficiency innovations, etc.). Yet again, as seen in Figure I-4, the best performers were 100% Leaders. For this factor, Challenge and Connection seemed about equally important.

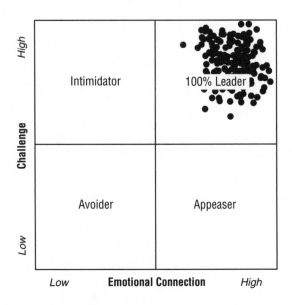

Figure I-4

The results seem pretty clear. If you push people but you don't seem to care about them, you're not going to be very successful. If you care about people but not enough to push them to become Hundred Percenters, you're not going to be very successful. But if you care enough about your folks to push them beyond what even they think they're capable of (i.e., you're a 100% Leader), you will succeed.

The age-old question plaguing leaders is whether it's better to be loved or feared. What our research seems to suggest is that while fear doesn't lead to superior results, it's also true that if being loved means you don't push people, that's not so great either. The balance seems to be that leaders should be loved, but they should be loved for pushing people to give 100%, not for coddling or appeasing them.

Test This Yourself

I'm happy for you to test the need for both challenge and connection yourself. Let me share a brief survey we did, and then I invite you to take it for yourself. We wanted to see if this idea made intuitive sense, without having to subject people to a stats lecture, and so we wrote a description of what it would be like to work for each style of leader, as follows:

> *Working for the Appeaser.* You're given enjoyable assignments, you're allowed to spend most of your time on work that plays to your strengths, your boss gives you lots of positive feedback, and your boss seems to care most about making sure you're really happy.
>
> *Working for the Intimidator.* You're given seemingly impossible assignments; you don't feel like you've got all the skills you need to complete those assignments; when your boss gives you feedback, it's usually pretty harsh and critical; and your boss seems to care most about achieving his goals no matter who's with him at the end.
>
> *Working for the Avoider.* Your boss doesn't really force too many assignments on you, you're not really required to learn new skills, your boss lets you figure out for yourself how you're doing, and your boss seems to care most about not getting in your way.
>
> *Working for the 100% Leader.* You're given really challenging assignments, you're required to learn new skills even in areas you might not consider to be your natural strengths, your boss gives you lots of constructive and positive

feedback, and your boss seems to care most about pushing you to maximize every ounce of your potential.

We wanted to see how people would evaluate each style, so we asked 3,000 random people (not paying clients) a series of questions about whom they wanted to work for. We asked questions like . . .
Which leader would you choose if you wanted:

A deeply fulfilling job?
A job you would be proud to tell your children about?
A job where you would grow as a professional?
A job where you would grow as a person?
The greatest chance of career success?
The greatest chance of achieving great things?
To maximize your full potential?

In every single case, more than 70% of respondents chose the 100% Leader. There are exceptions, of course, but generally speaking, people don't want to work for jerks, and they also don't want to be coddled all day.

To be fair, when we asked the question, "Which leader would you choose if you wanted a fun job?" the Appeaser garnered 56% of the votes. And that's a deep philosophical decision every leader is going to have to make: Is your job to make work fun, or is it to make work fulfilling and enriching and ultimately to position people to achieve great results?

You can download the full list of test questions at www.leader shipiq.com and take it yourself. If you give the test in a group setting, a fascinating exercise is to have everybody answer the questions and then discuss *why* you made your respective choices. What aspects of the 100% Leader, or the Appeaser, or the Intimidator, or the Avoider really appealed to you? And did your responses change depending on whether the question was about fun or ful-fillment or great achievement?

The Lure of Appeasers

Not for one second do I presume everyone is convinced that being a Hundred Percenter is a moral imperative. There are people who aren't sure words like "100%," "fist pump," "blood, sweat, and tears," and "greatness" belong in the same sentence as "work" and "job."

There are those who believe work is not the place to "make a dent in the universe," as Steve Jobs, founder of Apple, would say. There are those people who believe that if we can get our employees to be satisfied or even engaged, "We've done our job." Just get people to do a pretty good job, to care about their coworkers, to get some enjoyment out of their work, and to feel like their opinions count, and "Voila! We've done all that we really need to do." And there are those who believe leadership is more about making people happy and engaged than it is about making people great.

Think about the typical employee survey, for example. This is a pretty good barometer of what executives think is important. After all, every question executives ask employees is a reflection of the executives' core values. A typical survey asks employees whether their boss cares about them as people, if they have friends at work, if someone encourages their development, and whether they have opportunities to grow. It might even ask if they're satisfied.

But when was the last time you saw an employee survey that asked whether the boss pushed employees to give 100%, whether they actually gave 100%, and whether their goals were sufficiently challenging? And rather than asking whether employees were sat-isfied (which is a dully mediocre achievement), how about asking whether employees felt deeply fulfilled and as though they were maximizing their potential. (It should be noted that our employee survey [called the Hundred Percenter Index] does ask these 100% questions and more. In fact, it's how we were able to make the initial discovery about the 100% difference.)

Appeasement seems easy, as it doesn't ruffle feathers. What employee is going to get really mad if you say, "Our goal this year is to make every employee engaged and happy"? It's satisficing to fulfill the minimum requirements necessary to achieve a goal. By contrast, pushing someone to give 100% is hard work; it requires caring about that person, interacting with him or her, setting lofty goals, giving feedback, and lots more.

But what are the payoffs? Well, as I shared earlier, 100% Leaders generate better everything—profit, retention, innovation. But even more than that, when they help their folks become Hundred Percenters, greatness is possible. Hundred Percenters achieve more (like all those who produce great creations of art, science, and commerce throughout history). And they're more deeply fulfilled—after all, who feels more fulfilled: people who slide by without breaking a sweat or people who give their all and achieve something they might not even have thought possible before they started?

And what do Appeasers bring us? Missed opportunities, mostly. During the go-go 1990s, did we use our financial surpluses to fix education or health care, or to address critical future staffing shortages in engineering or nursing? Nope, that would have been too hard. After the attacks of September 11, 2001, did we take the opportunity to create another Greatest Generation? Nope, go shopping was the edict. In the economic expansion that followed, lasting until 2007, did we take the opportunity to address any more of those future financial problems, like social security or our abysmal personal savings rate? Nope, leverage, baby, leverage was our motto. And here's the real kicker: our overall happiness has not improved since 1950. While we've been appeasing ourselves under the guise of making ourselves happier, the great irony is that we're not actually any happier.

On a recent trip to train leaders at Microsoft, I found myself in front of a room of leaders I hadn't worked with before. Because these folks knew me only by reputation and weren't entirely sure what to expect, I knew I wouldn't engage them by launching into an inundating litany of leadership tactics. Instead, I asked them to do the following exercise: "Remember a time from any period in your life when a leader (boss, teacher, mentor, friend, etc.) inspired you to achieve something that was significant and deeply meaningful. Vividly describe what, specifically, the leader did that inspired you."

The responses I got told stories about leaders ranging from a crusty old high school football coach to Bill Gates himself. The stories were interesting, but the specifics paled in comparison to two common threads woven throughout each: one was an inspiring leader who pushed the "inspiree" past any doubts and limitations, and the other was a takeaway sense of pride. The participants beamed as they relayed the experiences. And over and over I heard phrases like "I never worked so hard in my life" and "I never thought I'd pull it off."

If we didn't have real challenges to tackle, the consequences of appeasement would be less severe. The problem is, we do have challenges, very big, very real challenges that demand more of leaders and employees than just "let's be engaged" or "happy" or "satisfied."

If ever there was a 100% Leader, it was Abraham Lincoln. In his Gettysburg Address, Lincoln said:

> It is rather for us to be here dedicated to the great task remaining before us—that from these honored dead we take increased devotion to that cause for which they gave the last full measure of

devotion—that we here highly resolve that these dead shall not have died in vain—that this nation, under God, shall have a new birth of freedom—and that government of the people, by the people, for the people, shall not perish from the earth.

Just look at those words. The speech is about the scope and intensity of the challenge we're going to tackle and our indefatigable commitment to meeting that challenge. Now imagine Lincoln was being counseled by today's experts on employee engagement (aka Appeasers). He might have said this instead: "Folks, we have a job before us, but don't worry about that because it's more important that you know that I really care about you and that I want you to lead lives with friends and that you wake up every day with the opportunity to be really satisfied and do what you're already good at without having to push yourself too hard."

I shudder to think where we'd be today if Lincoln had been an Appeaser instead of a 100% Leader. Of course, Neville Chamberlain was an Appeaser (remember the British prime minister who "negotiated" with Hitler and declared that "we have achieved peace for our time"?), Thankfully, he was replaced by Winston Churchill, a 100% Leader, who said, "Whatever the cost may be, we shall fight on the beaches, we shall fight on the landing grounds, we shall fight in the fields and in the streets, we shall fight in the hills; we shall never surrender."

Yes, 100% Leaders push us hard. But when they do, they teach us something about ourselves. They help us achieve extraordinary things. And they give us real opportunities for deep and lasting fulfillment. Companies like Google, Apple, Microsoft, GE, Southwest, the Ritz-Carlton, and Wegmans manage to achieve significant performance while still being fulfilling places to work. They invent and deliver exceptional products and services while setting new standards. And they do it with the knowledge that a whole new generation of 100% Leaders and companies is coming right behind them.

Can You Give 100% Forever?

Being a 100% Leader is fulfilling, and it's fulfilling to be a Hundred Percenter, but it also takes some work. So it's natural to ask, "Can people really keep this up forever?" I'll give you my honest answer: I don't know. We don't yet have 20 years of data to say definitively one way or the other. But let me offer an example that may lead us closer to an answer.

Bill Gates is a 100% Leader, and he's been that way since the start of his professional career. Now it's true he's no longer as big a presence at Microsoft as he once was. But in his philanthropy, he's ever the Hundred Percenter. In fact, it's entirely possible that as a result of his 100% Leadership in areas like reforming education or stopping the spread of AIDS, he will have an even bigger impact on the world than he did as the founder of Microsoft.

Maybe it's the case that 100% Leaders and Hundred Percenters can work on only one topic for so long. Maybe after a few decades, they need to change gears and tackle new challenges. But as I look at the world, I see lots of Bill Gateses (albeit sometimes on a smaller scale). They're people who can't stop being Hundred Percenters. They may have left a company, or the corporate world altogether, but they're tackling their new challenges with the same intensity of challenge and connection as they did their previous endeavors.

It's hard to abandon your quest for greatness once you've gotten a taste. Once you've realized that limitations are more fluid than fixed, that the deepest fulfillment comes from climbing the highest mountains, it's hard to go back to satisficing. When you experience the fulfillment and achievement that comes from giving 100%, it seems like it's difficult to go back to giving anything less.

In This Book

In this book, we're going to show how to become a 100% Leader. You'll learn how to challenge and connect with your people to help them become Hundred Percenters. Here's how the book will unfold.

Chapter 1: Set HARD Goals

If you want people to give 100%, they first need to know *what* they're giving 100% to achieve, *why* that's important and meaningful, and *how* they'll benefit. People want to know their work contributes to achieving something meaningful and significant. But you can't expect them to get there on their own; you've got to tell them. Otherwise, you can bet they're going to ask "Why?" "Why am I doing this?" "Why am I this cog and not another?" "Why is the wheel turning so slowly?" Or employees may not ask any questions at all. They may simply opt to find another organization that gives them the sense of purpose they want.

If you look behind the scenes at every truly great accomplishment, you'll find a challenging goal—a goal that tried and tested people's beliefs about what was possible. In this chapter, you'll learn how to set HARD (Heartfelt, Animated, Required, and Difficult) goals. These are goals that set the bar high, inspire greatness, and are difficult enough that we'll have to break a sweat to achieve them.

Chapter 2: Create Accountability with Constructive Feedback

People make mistakes, and they sometimes fail to achieve their 100% potential. There will be times when you need to provide some corrective feedback in order to make it better. But people don't tolerate getting scolded or corrected with a blunt analysis of the problem, especially when they don't get the corrective feedback that will help them to do better the next time. If you say something like, "Tim, your organizational skills are terrible; do something about it," you might feel like you're pushing that person because you gave him "tough feedback," but you're not going to inspire the performance change you want. Equally ineffective are popular softening "tricks" such as "criticize the action, not the person" or "layer the critical feedback with praise to make it sound kinder and gentler."

In this chapter, readers learn a six-step process called IDEALS that allows 100% Leaders to deliver tough feedback by lowering people's "walls of defensiveness" and preparing them to hear and assimilate the corrective feedback. This exciting technique gives leaders who might otherwise be hesitant to offer corrective feedback the wherewithal to do so effectively. And for leaders who offer feedback so tough that it becomes ineffective, they'll learn how to deliver feedback that inspires people to try again, pushing themselves the full 100%.

Chapter 3: Reclaim Our Heroes with Positive Reinforcement

Correcting people when they fall short is a necessary strategy for improving performance. But so too is positively reinforcing people when they *do* give 100%. One of our surveys showed that receiving positive reinforcement is one of the top predictors of achieving really difficult goals. Yet only 39% of employees say their boss does a good job of recognizing and acknowledging their accomplishments.

Positive reinforcement does not mean lavishing praise and rewarding people for menial achievements (like showing up for work on time). Rather, positive reinforcement is a tool to be used with laserlike precision to identify and reward behaviors that truly represent the 100% ideal. Readers will see the science of human motivation distilled into a system for providing meaningful, specific, and timely feedback that maximizes motivational impact and encourages even more 100% behavior.

Chapter 4: Stop Demotivating and Start Motivating

There's no such thing as one size fits all when it comes to keeping employees brimming with the kind of passion necessary for them to keep giving 100% effort. There's also a great deal of confusion about what people find motivating: 89% of managers believe that money is the biggest reason employees quit. But a whopping 91% of employees surveyed say money had nothing to do with their decision to leave an organization. Some people want certain hours or more flexibility. For others it is better benefits or more cash in their pockets. Some want career advancement, whereas others want to do their current job without being pushed to climb any higher. And even the best talent can stop giving 100% when they can't stand their boss or they dislike their coworkers.

In this chapter, readers will learn how to identify employees' Shoves (what demotivates employees and causes them to stop giving 100%) and Tugs (what excites them and inspires them to go above and beyond). We've created a script of Shoves and Tugs questions that allows leaders to find out what excites employees and elicits their 100% passion and also what is likely to drain their enthusiasm and cause them to turn a deaf ear to 100% leadership.

Chapter 5: 100% Skills with 0% Attitude

We call them Talented Terrors. They're the employees who have the 100% skills you want but with an attitude that is in the single digits. Not only do these folks make your life a living hell, but they also have a substantial negative impact on everyone who works for and interacts with your organization.

In our studies, we put skilled people with bad attitudes under the microscope. Then we used our findings to create a set of easy-to-use management tools that will teach readers how to give feedback that forces Talented Terrors to be accountable for their bad attitudes, induces Talented Terrors to voluntarily want to stop their bad behaviors (and minimize the toxic impact they can have on your great employees), and taps even deeper into their skills to help them fully realize their 100% potential.

Appendix: Why 5-Point Scales Don't Work (and Other Problems with Employee Surveys)

Employee surveys are powerful tools for assessing exactly what needs to be done to create a Hundred Percenter workplace. But all too often, these surveys are incorrectly used and become destructive forces that send both leaders and employees spiraling backward on the path to success. The Appendix offers some of the best-practice discoveries Leadership IQ has made about how to conduct employee surveys so that they guarantee positive and useful results.

Factors explored include the ineffectiveness of the typical 5-point rating scale, commonly used survey questions that provide zero positive benefit, the necessity of training managers to efficiently deal with survey results, the number of questions it really takes to get the needed information, strategies for avoiding mediocrity, and the relationship between timeliness and survey effectiveness. In addition to the foibles of employee surveys, I draw on two years of study results that use our 7-point scale Hundred Percenter Index to show how employee surveys can be used to take employees from ordinary to extraordinary.

Conclusion

If ever there was a time for 100% Leaders, this is it. It's a challenging world, and there will be times that Appeasing, Intimidating, and Avoiding will seem like attractive options.

One of Leadership IQ's more famous studies found that after a manager conducts a layoff, the most common leadership approach he or she takes with the remaining employees is Avoidance (after all, who really wants to hang out with a group of anxious, angry, and shocked employees who are going to ask lots of questions that can't be answered). But when leaders Avoid, bad things happen: 74% of employees who kept their job amid a corporate layoff say their own productivity has declined since the layoff. And 69% say the quality of their company's product or service has declined since the layoff.

Many historians have argued that great leaders required great challenges. Well, folks, we've got our challenges. Whether you're a world leader, supply chain manager at a small start-up, Fortune 500 executive, or nurse manager at a community hospital, you've got no shortage of great challenges. You can't Avoid, Intimidate, or Appease your way through them. But if you're willing to challenge and connect with your people like never before, to be a 100% Leader, we can create a world that we'll be proud to leave to our children.

1

Set HARD Goals

Introduction

People who are 100% Leaders achieve greatness by pushing past the comfort zone and inspiring their followers to do the same. Consider Oprah Winfrey, the daughter of an impoverished teenage mother in rural Mississippi, who today is one of the most influential women in the world; Jaime Escalante, a teacher who captured the minds of "unteachable" inner-city kids and filled them with the knowledge needed to pass the AP Calculus exam; and John F. Kennedy, who rallied the support of a frightened nation to put a man on the moon. If you look behind the scenes at every great accomplishment, you'll find a challenging goal that tried and tested people's beliefs about what was possible. You'll also find a person or people who weren't afraid to meet, or even surpass, that challenge.

And yet, notwithstanding the near perfect correlation between great achievements and challenging goals, our daily lives are nearly void of aspirations that test our limits and grow our character. The reasons why are plenty. We're intimidated by ambitious, challenging, difficult goals. We run the risk of resistance when we put great demands on people's time, energy, and talents. We fear that employees might interpret challenges that ask for more as an accusation that their performance to date has been inadequate. Tough goals could expose weaknesses and a lack of preparation. And, of course, unequivocal expectations for greatness beg the question, "What if we fail?" And that question, in turn, forces consideration of some deeply uncomfortable choices.

Demanding more of ourselves and one another is scary in an era where Happiology is our planetary religion and "Don't do today what you can put off till tomorrow" is our planetary slogan. We throw roadblocks in front of 100% Leaders who would otherwise test our limits. No goal can be approved until every resource is allocated, every milestone clarified, every assumption tested, every participant vetted, every response anticipated, every market researched, and every skill developed.

We may be afraid of challenge, but ironically, companies generally don't die because they tackled a challenge that was too big or they pushed themselves too hard. In virtually every major business failure, adhering to the status quo was the motivation behind the undoing. Kodak didn't meet the challenge when Fuji attacked, nor did Sears when Wal-Mart attacked. The Big Three automakers have made sticking to the status quo an art form (whether it's union contracts or high oil prices, they never met a tough challenge they couldn't duck or postpone). How many different companies were "status quo-ing" themselves to death when Google first emerged? Or Amazon? Or Southwest? Or Microsoft? Or Dell? Or Yamaha? Or Honda? (Please note, some of these companies now face significant challenges. So ask yourself, are they in trouble because they challenged themselves too much or because they became enamored with their own success and stopped looking for greater challenges?)

Before the financial meltdown started in 2008, we had years of prosperity. But we didn't "think big" and push ourselves to sacrifice and grow. We didn't view our economic prosperity as an investment pool that, spent wisely, could fund breakthrough innovations and solve what we knew were looming problems (health care, social security, a crumbling education system, global warming, etc.). Instead, we went shopping. We focused on feeling good rather than doing good. We counted our resources instead of developing our resourcefulness.

Even the financial collapse itself was a form of embracing the status quo. "Smile and take the money" became our financial ethic. Rating agencies didn't push themselves to learn the math that would have allowed them to actually do their jobs and accurately "rate" assets, nor did banks. How many financial executives sat down and pushed themselves to understand David Li's Gaussian copula function (the formula that allowed hugely complex risks to be modeled with seemingly more accuracy than ever before) so they might understand the formula's destructive potential? How many homeowners built financial plans around disciplined savings instead of miraculously, and irrationally, appreciating housing prices?

Yes, companies with challenging goals do fail. But it's rarely the goal itself that causes the failure. Rather, the failure occurs in communicating, executing, or resourcing the goal. What's more, companies with the guts to set challenging goals that are bigger than themselves typically have the cultural constitution to pick themselves up from failure and start again.

Overcoming Inertia

It would be great if employees spontaneously turned into Hundred Percenters without any help, like an amoeba reproducing through mitosis. But they don't; they need an outside push. Remember your high school or college physics class and Newton's first law of motion: an object at rest tends to stay at rest, and an object in motion tends to stay in motion with the same speed and in the same direction unless acted upon by an unbalanced force. Apply that law to your employees, and it says they will keep doing what they're doing—unless you do something about it.

As a 100% Leader, you already know that being a Hundred Percenter is significantly more fulfilling than squeaking by. When we do only what's required, or less, we incur untold personal, organizational, and societal costs. But unless your employees have been convincingly presented with these facts in a way that speaks of the benefits in words they can hear, they have no reason to stray from the path of the status quo.

Imagine you have your legs crossed (you're kicking back and reading this book, and you just happen to have your legs crossed). As long as crossing your legs is a comfortable position, you're likely to keep them crossed. Now imagine that out of nowhere, your legs suddenly cramp, and crossing them becomes deeply uncomfortable. What would you do? (This is not a trick question.) Of course, you'd uncross your legs. Without the leg cramp, the status quo of crossed legs would remain. However, make the status quo uncomfortable, and the old state is replaced by something new (and ostensibly better).

The first critical lesson of being a 100% Leader is that if the status quo felt bad, people would have changed already. So we can infer that if employees haven't yet changed to Hundred Percenter performance, they must think the status quo is A-OK.

Unfortunately, it's not just a lack of discomfort that attracts us to the status quo, it's also the fragility of our egos. Whatever our current state may be, we arrived here by virtue of thousands of decisions made along the way. Every project where we had a choice of the hard way or the easy way, work late or leave early, take a risk or play it safe, led us to where we are today. And presumably, we feel pretty good about the decisions we made.

If you come right out and tell an employee to change the state he or she is in, in effect you're saying, "Undo all those decisions you made previously because it turns out that they were bad decisions." It gets even worse if up until now you've approached employee motivation primarily by appeasing employees: coddling, loving 'em up, and telling them they're doing a great job. Conquering the ego is risky business. If you suddenly throw the present system into reverse, you're going to make heads spin, and that's counterproductive. Creating Hundred Percenters doesn't mean pulling the rug out from under your people. Instead, you need to give them a whole new platform on which to stand.

Setting HARD Goals

You don't have to be the bad guy who tears down your people in order to build them back up to something bigger and better. You can start from right where you are—if you're willing to set goals that challenge and inspire. Of course, we currently have goal-setting methodologies galore. There isn't a company in existence that hasn't set its share of SMART goals (most commonly defined as "Specific," "Measurable," "Achievable," "Realistic," and "Time-bound"). And most managers have gone through extensive training on the mechanics of constructing cogent goals.

But SMART goals can still be pretty dumb. Too often they act as impediments to, not enablers of, bold action and actually encourage mediocre and poor performance. "Hold on a minute," SMART goals seem to say. "Don't push beyond your resources; don't bite off more than you can chew; play it safe and stay within your limitations." Maybe if we weren't so focused on making sure our SMART goals were written correctly on our goal-setting forms, we might ask, "Is this goal fundamentally wimpy?"

A well-written goal may prevent you from being too impulsive, but when's the last time it stopped you, or anyone on your team, from copping out? Most organizations are pretty good at filling out forms correctly. What we're less adept at is making sure the content on those forms is gutsy and challenging enough to result in something great.

By the way, I've never met a CEO who didn't want his or her managers to be more innovative and proactive. Now ask yourself: is asking your managers to write goals using a color-by-numbers approach on a little form really going to unleash their innovative spirit? Isn't this as hypocritical as holding a painfully wasteful meeting to launch a new initiative to improve efficiency? Don't great leaders sometimes write their goals in speeches or memos or presentations or pictures or even on the backs of napkins? When it comes to setting goals, we might do well to concentrate less on the form and more on the content.

After years of studying Hundred Percenters and the 100% Leaders who enable them, Leadership IQ has distilled the critical success factors into a goal-setting methodology called HARD goals. Rather than making sure your goals fall within the realm of the eminently achievable, HARD goals push all the people involved beyond their current self-imposed restraints (and help them discover where their limits, if any, really exist).

To be effective, HARD goals must be . . .

Heartfelt (they exist to serve something bigger than
    ourselves)
Animated (they're so vividly described and presented that to
    not reach them would leave us wanting)
Required (they're as critical to our continued existence as
    breathing and water)
Difficult (they're so hard they'll test every one of our limits)

There are leaders who are already very good at setting HARD goals. You'll recognize some of the better-known 100% Leaders by their reputations for inspiring others to become Hundred Per-centers. The HARD goal in Abraham Lincoln's Gettysburg Address steeled our resolve to fight so that "government of the people, by the people, for the people, shall not perish from the earth." John F. Kennedy's HARD goal asked the nation to "commit itself to achieving the goal, before this decade is out, of landing a man on the moon and returning him safely to the earth." Ronald Reagan's HARD goal demanded "Mr. Gorbachev, tear down this wall!" Winston Churchill's HARD goal made clear that "whatever the cost may be, we shall fight on the beaches, we shall fight on the landing grounds, we shall fight in the fields and in the streets, we shall fight in the hills; we shall never surrender."

You don't have to be a world leader to issue a HARD challenge. Nor do you have to have thousands of followers. You just have to be willing to push past what's easy—to do what's right.

I'm not a natural runner. For most of my life, I wouldn't run even if chased. However, a few years ago, my wife (who ran cross-coun-try growing up) issued me a HARD goal of running a marathon. It wasn't easy (each step hurt a little more than the previous one), it wasn't pretty (imagine a sausage with feet), and it sure as heck wasn't fast (over five hours). As part of the training, I once did a four-hour run on a treadmill (which probably hurt worse than the actual race). I also gave up hours of comfortably sitting on my butt on my couch (and I've got a really comfortable couch) during football season.

On any given day, if you had asked me if sitting on my couch watching TV would make me happier than running, I'd have said yes. And if you had totaled up every one of those days during my two-year training period, my "happiness score" would mathemat-ically tilt in favor of sitting. But when the race was over, and the nausea passed, and I could walk again, if you had then asked me if I were a better person for running a marathon, had discovered an inner strength, had learned that a lack of natural talent should never be an excuse for avoiding a challenge, had become less fearful of big challenges, had acquired more character and life lessons to offer my children, I would have resoundingly answered *yes*!

Admittedly, my marathon goal was pretty small compared with the other goals I mentioned above (although for an overweight, former smoker, perhaps I gave my children a few more years with their dad). But these are precisely the kinds of choices we face every day. We may never find ourselves sitting behind the same desk as Lincoln, Kennedy, Reagan, or Churchill. We may never be faced with decisions upon which rest millions of lives. But every business plan we write represents an opportunity. Every sales presentation, every customer interaction, every budget request, and every financial approval is a chance for us to push ourselves and our employees toward untold greatness.

Sure, we can take the easy way and do only what's minimally required, stonewall and hide behind the imposed constraints of our SMART goals, and encourage our people to do the same. Or we can decide to accept our responsibility and move beyond doing what's easy—to do what's right. To paraphrase our actor friends, there are no small decisions, only small deciders.

Let's get started making our own HARD goals.

Heartfelt

There's nothing inherently implausible about a CEO rolling out of bed in the morning, intrinsically motivated to go to the office and create shareholder wealth. And when one of his kids asks, "Will you be home in time for my soccer game tonight, Daddy?" the CEO could sincerely apologize and say, "I'm sorry little Billy, but thousands of people are counting on me to finish this report so their stock goes up and they have enough money to buy food and clothes."

Now, imagine the guy who works the line at that organization skipping into the office to create shareholder wealth. Or saying to little Billy, "I'm sorry, son, but Daddy has to weld three more parts so the company's stock price goes up by a millionth of a point, thus making some rich people just a little richer. And no, we won't see it, so don't ask for that new bike."

Money is great, and financial metrics have their place. But working for money will never be as motivating as working for something bigger than oneself. A few senior executives may be intrinsically charged up to boost share price, but the folks on the front lines need something more meaningful to want to become Hundred Percenters. And frankly, companies whose existential anchor is money (e.g., Enron) will never outperform a company whose existence is predicated on serving customers.

However, serving something bigger than money, or (gasp) bigger than ourselves, is really hard. Google says it very well in its corporate philosophy, which includes a list of "Ten things Google has found to be true." Here's number one on that list: "Focus on the *user* and all else will follow." Google goes on to say:

> From its inception, Google has focused on providing the best user experience possible. *While many companies claim to put their customers first, few are able to resist the temptation to make small sacrifices to increase shareholder value.* Google has steadfastly refused to make any change that does not offer a benefit to the users who come to the site:
>
> The interface is clear and simple.
>
> Pages load instantly.

Placement in search results is never sold to anyone.

Advertising on the site must offer relevant content and not be a distraction.

The italicizing above is mine, and it's there to make a point. Every company on earth puts the word "customer" or "patient" or "user" in its mission statement. It looks great embossed on a plaque hanging in the boardroom or lobby, but are we actually willing to put it into our goals? Would we make sacrifices to serve that customer, patient, user, or whomever we state as our higher purpose?

Companies that tend to make the most money over time do so by delivering the most value to somebody bigger than themselves, not by sacrificing the customer to immediately increase shareholder value. Sure, you can pop your stock for a quarter here or there through financial narcissism, but it will come back to bite you. Not only will your customers eventually revolt, but Hundred Percenters don't go above and beyond to serve a cause that is self-serving.

If you want to build a heartfelt higher purpose into your goals and inspire more Hundred Percenters, make your goals NOBLE. You can use the actual definition of NOBLE, or you can use it as an acronym, as follows:

*N*ame a party
*O*ther than ourselves who will
*B*enefit from this goal
*L*ike customers or
*E*nd users

See if you can find the Hundred Percenter who is working toward a NOBLE goal in this story: One day, a man came upon a construction site where three masons were working. He asked the first mason, "What are you doing?" The mason slapped down some mortar and said, "I'm laying bricks." The man then asked the second mason the same question, "What are you doing?" The mason shrugged and said, "I'm putting up a wall." Finally, the man approached the third mason, who was whistling as he worked. Once again, he asked, "What are you doing?" The mason stopped whistling, turned to him with a big smile, and said, "I'm building a cathedral."

Lest you think me a Pollyannaish babe in the woods of bare-knuckled corporate politics, let me offer this thought: if your goal is wrapped in the flag of NOBLE purpose, you're about as politically protected as you can be. If you give a speech launching a new initiative and you can demonstrate how it will be better for the customers, then who in his right mind is going to stand up and shout, "To heck with the customers; let's take the money for ourselves!" (Of course, there are those people who will do exactly that, but they will have politically kneecapped themselves with their narcissism.)

One word of caution: You can't play Machiavellian games and speak of NOBLE goals only to turn around and shaft the people or the causes you promised to serve. When you set truly NOBLE goals, you're obligating yourself to them. That's why, even though politicians have mastered the feigned indignation of champions fighting for something bigger than themselves, they're so distrusted. They talk a good game, but the Lincolns are few and far between.

Are Enemies NOBLE?

Most CEOs won't admit it, but having enemies is fun (in sports we call them rivals, and they're essential to ratings and revenue). Having people to benchmark against gets our competitive juices flowing. Enemies can feel like a NOBLE goal (we're not focused on ourselves; we're focused on killing those other people over there). But while competing against mortal enemies can elevate our performance, it's fraught with two dangers. First, killing our competitors is simply not as motivating as serving a more NOBLE aim. When you tell little Billy you're missing his soccer game, do you want to say it's because you had to destroy a competitor or because you had to serve a customer who was really counting on you and needed your help? The second problem with enemy goals is more practical: when you've beaten your enemy, whom do you fight next? To put it another way, where do you go when you get to number one?

Animated

When most people describe their goals (whether SMART goals or some other kind), they, and anyone listening, can barely stifle a yawn. When's the last time you got so jazzed about the thought of hitting your budget target that you actively fantasized about the exact moment you would present the results to the team?

There are many reasons why people don't get excited about their goals (for example, they're not challenging, meaningful, or vital to our survival). But one critical reason for our goal apathy is that our goals typically sound sterile. We may have a goal that says, "Finish and deliver the new X14 product to our biggest customer by the close of business in 73 days." Yes, it's specific and measurable and time-limited and all the rest. But inspirational? This goal isn't going to make anyone jump up and say, "Wow, I am going to sacrifice whatever is asked of me in order to achieve that! I will drip blood, sweat, and tears until I have given every ounce of strength to this cause."

Imagine if Martin Luther King, Jr., had stood on the steps of the Lincoln Memorial and said, "Our goal should be that within the next 30 years, the incidents of hate crimes will be reduced by 63% and that the percentage of minorities living below the poverty line will be no higher than the percentage for any other racial group." Those would be aspirational goals, to be sure. But inspirational? Not so much.

Let us be thankful that he instead said:

> I have a dream that one day on the red hills of Georgia, the sons of former slaves and the sons of former slave owners will be able to sit down together at the table of brotherhood.
>
> I have a dream that my four little children will one day live in a nation where they will not be judged by the color of their skin but by the content of their character.

HARD goals are aspirational. They force us to push through our self-imposed limitations, to focus on something bigger than our own immediate wants, and to solve challenges of vital necessity. But HARD goals are also inspirational. You may not naturally use the vivid imagery of a Martin Luther King, Jr., but there are specific tools that will help animate your goals and improve their inspirational quotient.

The key to creating an animated and inspirational HARD goal is to describe it so graphically that people can actually experience it (albeit in their minds) long before they actually achieve it. We're going to use the power of graphic imagery for two purposes. First, we're going to build an immensely powerful attachment to our goal in the minds of our employees; they're going to "feel" this goal heart and soul. Second, we're going to simulate our goal mentally so we can work out any logical problems with our goal and uncover any hidden landmines (before we hit them in real life).

Parenthetically, the most useful aspect of SMART goals has typically been the "M" (Measurable). What you'll find as you animate your goals is that you will be making your HARD goals measurable. But you won't just be making them numerically measurable (although that's a key component); you'll be making them behaviorally and emotionally measurable as well.

Picture in Your Mind's Eye

Whether we're talking about the kind of visualization that helps elite athletes perform under pressure or the guided imagery used by cancer patients to destroy their illness, the power of imagery has been documented in countless studies. A study in the *British Journal of Cancer* comparing two groups of female cancer patients found that patients who used imagery were more relaxed and had a higher self-rated quality of life during chemotherapy than patients who didn't use imagery. The imagery patients also had enhanced lymphokine-activated killer cytotoxicity, higher numbers of activated T cells, and reduced blood levels of tumor necrosis factor, which loosely translated means that they seemed healthier than the group not using imagery. Additionally, a study reported in *The Sport Psychologist* found that mental training techniques, including imagery, improved competitive triathlon performance.

Visualization (imagery) taps into our imagination. It encourages a mental rehearsal of the feeling of joy and satisfaction that beating the odds and reaching success will bring. This creates a strong emotional attachment to the outcome and gives us greater drive (a Hundred Percenter drive) to get there. Employees who are given a strong visual image of what the achievement of a goal will look like will be motivated to access everything they've got, including untapped potential, to make that vision real.

The best way to develop an animated description of your goal is to imagine what it will be like for the whole team when you hit your HARD goal. Describe exactly what's happening, how it feels, what the numbers are, who's saying what to whom, etc. You want that future moment to feel so real that when folks are done visualizing it, they actually feel a little disappointed that the moment is gone.

It's important to reiterate: begin by thinking about the end state, not your current state. If you were just to total up all the daily to-dos and extrapolate them into whatever time frame you've assigned to your goal, it's unlikely you'll inspire Hundred Percenter performance. You've got to mentally stretch yourself, free yourself from your daily constraints, and begin at the end.

In your visualization, address the following three key issues.

Outcomes

What specifically was achieved? This includes whatever metrics were achieved, but take it a step further. Instead of just saying, "Our project came in a month ahead of schedule," try helping your team look into the future and visualize the specific outcomes that you'll achieve: "Our project was submitted on March 13, which was 27 days ahead of schedule. We saved 8 of those days in the design phase, because unlike our past projects, we started on time, and we made our spec document deadline nonnegotiable. (It took an all-nighter, but it set the tone for the rest of the project.) We saved another 12 days during coding because we held a code-jam with 3 days off-site, locked away doing nothing but coding and talking about coding (and eating pizza and drinking coffee). The other 7 days we saved . . ." You get the idea.

The visualizations of your HARD goal outcomes will have far greater impact if you use absolute numbers instead of percentages. For example, rather than saying, "We came in 10% under budget," say, "We saved $873,000." Here's an interesting discovery we made that explains why absolute numbers are preferable. During a 6-month period, we tracked over 2,000 managers, all of whom made New Year's resolutions to lose weight. As you might guess, not a whole lot of weight was actually lost. But the people who expressed their weight-loss goals in absolute terms (e.g., lose 13 pounds) lost roughly 4 times more weight than those who expressed their goals in percentages (e.g., lose 5%).

It seems that, mentally, a real number is harder to dodge, while percentages give you an out. If you want to lose 5% (or cut 10% from your budget, etc.), you can always tweak the other half of the equation (you can cut 10% from $2 million, or $2.2 million, or $2.5 million). But when you say, "We're going to cut $217, 000," it doesn't matter if you're cutting it from $2 million or $3 million because your target is fixed. (Yes, anything can be gamed, but it's mentally harder when the number is absolute.)

And don't use round numbers (e.g., a multiple of 5 or 10). Round numbers seem to say, "I should cut something, but I don't really know how much and I haven't given it much thought, so I'll just use a nice round number." By contrast, nonround numbers indicate more actual thought was put into developing the goal, which increased the likelihood of actually achieving the goal. The moral is to be specific about the outcomes you want to achieve.

Actions
Back in the 1930s, the Walt Disney Studio came up with the idea of storyboarding its animations. These graphic organizers gained great popularity as a means of sharing with cast and crew the completed vision they were hired to create. Using a verbal form of storyboarding, 100% Leaders outline the actions that will bring a HARD goal to life. It may not be as captivating as a Disney animation, but when employees are given an animated presentation of the blow-by-blow steps they will take to achieve a goal, you will get a captive audience.

Here's an example of a leader who didn't do a very inspirational job of animating the actions required to achieve a HARD goal: "This is going to be our best quarter ever, but in order to get there, we've got to run our meetings more efficiently."

This certainly sounds hopeful, but it doesn't tell the listeners what they'll actually be doing to carry the action out.

Here's how a 100% Leader might express a more animated vision of the actions it will take to achieve the HARD goal: "As of this moment, we're done with meetings that eat up time and produce minimal results. Prior to every meeting, you will be receiving longer agendas than you have in the past. Everyone is accountable for knowing the information and coming to the meeting 100% prepared. We won't be stopping or backtracking to catch anyone up. We'll start with a statement of achievement so we know exactly what we're all there to accomplish. That leaves us with deciding who will do the tasks at hand and how, at which point the meeting will end."

Feelings

I strongly suspect the Wright brothers had a pretty clear picture of what it would feel like to fly before they succeeded in building an airplane that left the ground. That feeling of success, before it's achieved, is one of the main drivers behind Hundred Percenter effort. You can't dangle a HARD goal in front of your people and expect them to keep reaching for it if they have no idea what achieving it will feel like. Everyone has something to take away from bringing a HARD goal to life. Pinpoint what it is, and help your people visualize how great that moment of success will feel.

Animated goals are all about imagination and creativity. We've had clients throw goal-achievement parties for their employees at the launch of a HARD goal to help cement the imagery of the year-long challenge ahead. Other clients have premarked company calendars to "track" future achievements. Some clients have distributed mock articles that looked as if they were written up in *USA Today* to "document" future achievements. Others began a HARD goal by giving awards and a formal presentation, as though they all had already achieved their goals. Do what you can to make your HARD goal as graphic and desirable as possible.

Let's return briefly to Dr. King. Do you have a dream? Can you picture this dream, this goal, in your mind? How did achieving this goal look, smell, feel, taste, and sound? Who was there? What had to be done to get there? Write it all down. You might not come up with something quite as beautifully written as "I have a dream that my four little children will one day live in a nation where they will not be judged by the color of their skin but by the content of their character." But if you help people to really experience your goal, if you invite them to share in your dream, you too will inspire those people to sacrifice, achieve, and experience a deeper fulfillment than they would have otherwise imagined possible.

Required

At their essence, HARD goals ask people to push beyond their previously conceived limitations. In part, they do this by convincing people of the benefits of going above and beyond—"Imagine the deep sense of fulfillment you'll get from achieving an incredibly difficult goal in the service of something bigger than yourself." But a HARD goal does more than paint an attractive picture of something in the future. It also solves a deep-seated pain. HARD goals aren't just nice to do, they're necessary to do. So before you can expect full adoption of your HARD goals, you've got to help people understand why they're required.

When you assign a HARD goal that asks someone to become a Hundred Percenter, in effect, you're saying, "There's something wrong with what you're doing right now" or "I don't know what percent effort you're presently giving, but it ain't 100%." You might not actually say those exact words, but just the implication of "Let's aspire to this place that's bigger and better than where we are now" sends a clear message that the place presently inhabited is insufficient.

The natural reaction is to want to know why. "Why can't I just keep on doing what I'm doing?" "Why do I have to hit this new goal?" "Why do you think I'm not already giving 100%?" "Why do you think I should aim higher?" Before you can get full buy-in to a HARD goal, you have to answer those questions. If you don't, your goal will seem optional and insignificant. You want to send a message that says, "Achieving this goal is required; it's a necessary part of your existence." This is a message that will inspire someone to want make the shift from the status quo to Hundred Percenter.

How do you actually do this? Start by asking your employees if they can think of reasons why this goal is so necessary. You might try, "From your perspective, what consequences or repercussions do we face if we don't pursue this goal?" If you start by asking, rather than telling, employees will often surprise you with their insight. And if they can start to see for themselves why this new goal is absolutely required for our collective success and survival, their buy-in will be tremendous. Maybe you've heard the old joke: *Q:* How many psychologists does it take to screw in a lightbulb? *A:* Just one, but the lightbulb has to want to change.

Now, if your employees can't come up with good reasons, then you'll have to tell them. But you want to keep your reasoning very calm and matter-of-fact. When you cut to the core of most human communication, you're usually left with four main elements: Facts, Interpretation, Reaction, and Ends. Even though these four elements often come as a package deal, the mix can still be explosive. When the Facts (F) get tangled in the Interpretations, Reactions, and Ends (IRE), the result is FIRE, and nothing is more counterproductive to effective communication. Those who are 100% Leaders stay focused on the Facts and keep Interpretations, Reactions, and Ends (IRE; yes, usually the things that make us angry) as far away as possible.

People love to buy, but they hate to be sold. Shoving your personal agenda down someone else's throat accomplishes little besides making that person want to do completely the opposite. Buying into a HARD goal is an important decision, one that carries with it an element of personal risk. You're asking folks to change the way they think and act. Unlike IRE, Facts don't attempt to strong-arm decision making, they aren't egocentric, nor do they carry implied negative meaning. To the contrary, Facts provide neutral information that brings understanding and the power to draw independent conclusions.

You can easily test if your employees believe that this new goal is required. Ask your employees this question, "Do you believe this goal is necessary?" If 70% or more say yes, then you're in good shape. Any less than that, and you've still got some work to do.

What Happens If You Shortcut This Part?

It's a legitimate question, and one that's asked often: what happens if you haven't fully established why your HARD goal is required (i.e., why achieving this goal is a necessary part of your existence)? The answer is that you will come off sounding clueless. Which means your HARD goal doesn't stand a chance.

In 1961, President Kennedy gave a speech to a joint session of Congress to discuss his plans for putting a man on the moon. You probably remember the line, "I believe that this nation should commit itself to achieving the goal, before this decade is out, of landing a man on the moon and returning him safely to the earth." What you're probably less familiar with are the paragraphs that preceded that famous line. Here are some quotes worth noting:

. . . if we are to win the battle that is now going on around the world between freedom and tyranny, the dramatic achievements in space which occurred in recent weeks should have made clear to us all, as did the Sputnik in 1957, the impact of this adventure on the minds of men everywhere, who are attempting to make a determination of which road they should take.

Recognizing the head start obtained by the Soviets with their large rocket engines, which gives them many months of lead time, and recognizing the likelihood that they will exploit this lead for some time to come in still more impressive successes, we nevertheless are required to make new efforts on our own.

This is strong language. And it's very clear that we should *not* be happy and satisfied with our status quo. At the time Kennedy gave this speech, the United States was engaged in a fierce cold war with the Soviets, we were still reeling from the Bay of Pigs, and the nuclear threat was very real. (Children used to practice ducking under their desks in response to a nuclear attack. As much as we say we fear Al Qaeda today, my kids have never once practiced ducking under their desks in an anticipated response to a terrorist attack.)

Everything Kennedy said helped set the stage for his visionary line. The preceding paragraphs make us nervous and unhappy with the way things are. They wake us up and prepare us to hear the challenging goal that follows.

In contrast to this, in 2004, President George W. Bush delivered a speech at NASA to announce that "With the experience and knowle dge gained on the moon, we will then be ready to take the next steps of space exploration: human missions to Mars and to worlds beyond." Okay, we're going to aim for Mars just as we had previously aimed for the moon. There's just one problem: nowhere in this speech does the president explain *why* we need to go to Mars or *why* we should be dissatisfied with our present space efforts.

In the speech, President Bush tells us that we're proud of our space program, and he describes how it has revolutionized our understanding of the universe and produced technological advances that have benefited all humanity. Great stuff. But nowhere do we hear *why* we should care about space or Mars. Kennedy made it clear that the Soviets were gobbling up the planet, threatening our civilization, and that space was one area where we could really put a dent in their plans. But there's nothing even close to that in the Mars speech.

Unless you effectively answer why a goal is required, you will sound like you're coming out of left field when you start discussing the challenging goal. It should be noted that President Bush's speech was not well received. Not because it was poorly delivered or even because going to Mars was a bad idea. It was panned because the U.S. population asked, "Why the heck are we talking about Mars?" If people are left wondering why you're setting a HARD goal, you need to backtrack and bring them up to speed on why the HARD goal is required.

Difficult

Psychology professors Edwin Locke and Gary Latham, who could be called the fathers of goal-setting theory, radically altered how we think about goals. In the mid-1950s, it was thought that task difficulty had an inverse curvilinear relationship with performance. In other words, when goals were either too easy or too hard, people didn't perform well. But when goals were moderately difficult, people performed the best (see Figure 1-1).

However, as Locke and Latham refined the science in the 1960s and 1970s, they discovered a positive linear relationship between *difficulty* and *performance* (see Figure 1-2).

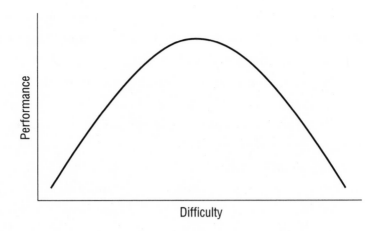

Figure 1-1

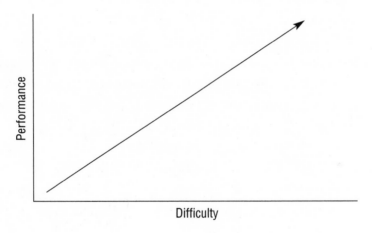

Figure 1-2

In study after study, they found that, on the whole, as the difficulty of the goal increased, performance also increased, given that the goal was specific. You couldn't just tell people to "do their best" on a really difficult goal, because when faced with this bit of management pabulum, those people chose *not* to do their best. But make the goal specific and hard, and you get results. Certainly, performance could be expected to drop when the true limits of one's ability are reached. But as I've noted, pushing people that hard is a pretty rare occurrence in the real world of work ("good enough" is much more common than "great").

Professors Miriam Erez and Isaac Zidon, inspired by Locke and Latham, conducted an experiment with 140 engineers. They administered seven trials of a perceptual speed test that required the engineers to determine how many digits or letters in a row were the same as the circled one to the left of each row (just imagine the kind of test that Mensa members do for fun). Each successive trial got harder, with a diminishing probability of success (objectively derived from previous experiments). The first trial had a 90% probability of success, the second trial had a 60% probability of success, then 30%, then 10%, then 2%, then 0.5% (that's half a percent probability), then 0% probability of success.

Before each trial started, participants were given a specific goal (e.g., find 10 instances of that character). Next, they were asked to acknowledge the goal and to rate their level of acceptance of the goal. Now, here's the crazy part: those people who openly accepted their goal had improved performance as the task got more difficult. Even when the probability of success was 2% or 0%, performance still improved. For those who moderately accepted their goal, performance also improved, even as the difficulty increased (they still did better when there was a 2% chance of success than when there was a 30% chance of success). And the people who didn't accept their goal had performance that got worse as the task got more difficult. But even here, performance didn't really fall off until the probability of success fell below 2%.

But, you might be thinking, wouldn't the smartest people be the most likely to accept this challenge? Hence what we're really measuring here is just whether smart people score better on tests. The answer is that it's always a distinct possibility that the people with the greatest abilities are more likely to accept tough challenges. However, in this case, the people with the lowest level of acceptance had the highest scores when the challenges were easiest. When there was a high probability of success, the low-acceptance people beat the high-acceptance people. How can the high-acceptance people be "smarter" when they just got beat by the low-acceptance people? And that didn't change until the difficulty of the challenge increased.

Still having doubts? OK, then you could respond, "Well the smart people didn't kick it up a notch until things got really tough, so you can't compare their scores during the easy trials." Perhaps, but if you're arguing that people respond only to really tough goals, then you're basically back to proving my original point: make your goal really hard.

We conducted our own study to see how people truly feel about HARD goals. We asked 4,200 of our subscribers a series of questions, including the following, and asked respondents to rate their answers on a 7-point scale:

"My boss pushes me harder than I would push myself."
"I will have to exert extra effort to achieve my assigned goals for this year."
"I will have to learn new skills to achieve my assigned goals for this year."

Guess what? Our regression analyses showed that as scores on these questions went up, so did scores on these four outcome questions:

"I consider myself a high performer."
"The work I do makes a difference in people's lives."
"I recommend this company to others as a great place for people to work."
"I recommend my boss to others as a great person to work for."

Our study shows that bosses who push employees harder than the employees would push themselves—who assign goals that require extra effort and skills development to succeed—have employees who like the boss and the company and who feel better about themselves and the work they do.

What's the explanation, you ask. Here are two. First, HARD goals instill confidence. Nobody would give HARD goals to a moron. You'd only give HARD goals to somebody who had a shot at achieving them. So, by extension, if your boss gives you a HARD goal, he or she must believe you can achieve it. And that is another way of the boss saying, "I believe in you; I trust you; you're the right person for this job." (You might be tempted to argue that your boss is just sadistic, but if HARD goals also make you feel good about yourself, a sadist would avoid HARD goals for fear of improving your self-esteem.)

Second, HARD goals convey that your work is important. Nobody would spend the time or energy to create HARD goals for work that was non-value-added (aka dumb, wasteful, etc.). "You know that report we produce that nobody ever reads, that gets produced only because a hundred years ago the founder used to like to verify the calculations from his abacus; you know the report I mean? Well let's convene a team with a goal of making this dumb report take 10 minutes instead of 20. It will test the very limits of kindergarten math and data entry typing, but let's go for it!" Puh-lease.

How Difficult Is Difficult?

Please don't misunderstand me: I'm not saying that you can't create a goal that is so impossible that it becomes demotivating. Of course you could set such an absurd goal (and every so often we run across a truly impossible, and thus demotivating, goal). Rather, what I'm really saying is that we have less to fear from goals that are too hard than we do from goals that are not hard enough. Why? Because there is such an enormous headwind pushing against anyone who tries to create really difficult goals (let alone goals that might be "too difficult") that they're just not very common.

So how hard should you make your goal? Notwithstanding all these great studies, in the world outside of the laboratory, estimating the difficulty of a goal is, well, difficult. So here's a quick test to help you figure out if your HARD goals are hard enough. Start by assessing the goals you've assigned in the past year (they can be annual goals, project goals, specific assignments, etc.).

> Test #1: Ask your employees what new skills (if any) they had to learn to achieve these goals.

If they aren't learning all sorts of new skills, then your goals are probably not hard enough. Try making your goals 30% harder (also see the section that follows on the effect of a lack of resources) and then evaluate again in three months. Otherwise, if employees have learned a lot, move on to Test #2.

> Test #2: Ask your employees if, at the outset, they knew they could achieve these goals.

HARD goals are scary and force us to question our abilities. So if your employees knew they could accomplish the goals before they even started, try making your goals 20% harder and then evaluate again in three months.

The Universal Test: Pay Close Attention

The previous tests are designed based on our experience advising thousands of leaders. But the most important experience is really your own. Watch and interact with your employees. See where they're breaking down; look for signs that they're really sweating to accomplish the goals you set; be hypervigilant for cleverness and innovation. If you pay enough attention, you should be able to tell if they're pushing or just coasting.

(A Lack of) Resources Can Increase Difficulty

There's an old adage many advertising agencies live by: you can have it cheap, fast, or good—pick two. Knowing that everyone wants all three, they use this line to justify higher billings (you gripe because you want all three; they relent and say, "OK, but it'll cost you." You feel vindicated and open the checkbook). Our research shows that if you're smart, you can pay for two and still get all three, and without any haggling. Nothing makes a goal more challenging than constrained resources. When pushed, folks tend to find creative ways to make cheap and fast projects with good quality. Or they find ways to make fast and good projects come in under budget. And so on. In other words, they become Hundred Percenters.

As crazy as it sounds, limiting peoples' resources can actually be an effective way to grow their skills and elevate their performance. There are four major categories—or buckets—of resources that we can give people:

1. Formal Authority (being able to allocate resources, change schedules, punish or reward, etc.)
2. Skills (knowledge to achieve the goal, including preexisting skills, formal education, training, etc.)
3. Budget (money, including expenses, labor, overtime, capital, equipment, etc.)
4. Time (how long they have to complete the goal)

A few years ago, I launched a task force within Leadership IQ to focus solely on researching start-ups and entrepreneurs. When we analyzed their resources (whether bootstrapped or venture funded), we found that virtually all the successful start-ups were slightly underresourced. Specifically, they were short in one of the four resource buckets above. Interestingly, when start-ups were fully resourced (i.e., they had all the money, authority, skills, and time they needed), their results weren't as good. Of course, as anyone who's ever worked on a creative project can attest, oftentimes the best work occurs under constrained conditions (in other words, necessity is the mother of invention).

But constrained resources do not enjoy a monotonic relationship with success. When these companies were seriously underresourced (i.e., they were short in two or more of those resource buckets), their performance suffered. Over and over we saw that a company could be short of time or money or authority or skills and still deliver great performance. However, when they were short two or more of those resources, their performance suffered.

Our first major insight was that just the right amount of resource deprivation can actually improve results. Too many resources, and we're too fat and happy to push ourselves. Too few resources, and it's like trying to climb Mt. Everest without boots or gloves.

Our second major insight occurred when we looked at how these start-ups responded to resource deprivation. Not only did missing one resource bucket heighten their resourcefulness, but typically it also forced them to develop a new set of skills.

When people were deprived of Formal Authority, they became more skilled at influencing others and using "soft power" to accomplish their goals.

When people were deprived of sufficient Skills, they pushed themselves to acquire new aptitudes. For example, we saw programmers learn new languages, scientists enter new disciplines, and artists become financial wizards, all in the name of accomplishing a challenging goal.

When people were deprived of Budget, they became very clever at doing without or creating inventive financing mechanisms. When we interviewed venture capitalists and private equity investors, they identified this skill as one of their most prized when evaluating entrepreneurs.

When people were deprived of Time, they learned how to work faster, manage projects better, and become ruthlessly efficient at managing themselves and others.

Strategy gurus Gary Hamel and C. K. Prahalad identified the power of scarce resources in their classic 1993 *Harvard Business Review* article:

> If modest resources were an insurmountable deterrent to future leadership, GM, Philips, and IBM would not have found themselves on the defensive with Honda, Sony, and Compaq. NEC succeeded in gaining market share against AT&T, Texas Instruments, and IBM despite an R&D budget that for most of its history was more modest in both absolute and relative terms than those of its rivals. Toyota developed a new luxury car for a fraction of the resources required by Detroit. IBM challenged Xerox in the copier business and failed, while Canon, a company only 10% the size of Xerox in the mid-1970s, eventually displaced Xerox as the world's most prolific copier manufacturer. CNN in its adolescence managed to provide 24 hours of news a day with a budget estimated at one-fifth that required by CBS to turn out 1 hour of evening news.

While we've had this insight for decades, companies still get killed standing motionless, afraid to move until they've mobilized every resource that could possibly, in some rare contingency, ever be needed. Fortunately, behemoths like Microsoft aggressively try to maintain their start-up culture. They eschew the trappings of bureaucracy as much as possible (they have fewer administrative personnel than most companies their size), and if a project requires five people to complete it, they typically assign four.

Conclusion

HARD goals are . . . hard. They present challenges that test our limits and build our character, but the benefits are many. HARD goals make us better, stronger, wiser—something more than we were before we embraced the challenge.

To motivate employees to give Hundred Percenter effort to HARD goals, 100% Leaders make the goals:

Heartfelt
Animated
Required
Difficult

What follows is a HARD goal memo, written by the CEO of ChocoBot Inc., the world's largest maker of edible jewelry (licorice bracelets, chocolate watches, gummy broaches, etc.). ChocoBot's products are sold through specialty candy stores. The company is fictitious, but the goals are drawn from dozens of companies' very real HARD goals. (I made the company fictitious and kind of funny to prevent the typical trap of "They're not like us" defensiveness, thereby making it easier to absorb the lessons of HARD goals.)

The important thing to note about this memo is how the CEO animates the future with goals that are difficult, heartfelt, and essential to the company's survival in order to inspire his people to strive for Hundred Percenter greatness. Sure, the CEO is facing a tough economy. But there is no backing off here; it's pedal-to-the-metal, full speed ahead!

To All Employees:

Let me begin by stating the obvious: times are tough. The edible jewelry market is down 6%, chocolate sales overall in our sector are down 5%, and positive press mentions about the health benefits of chocolate are down more than 40% from a year ago. It's rough out there, and that's precisely why we're going to leapfrog past every one of our competitors. We're going to think big, we're going to do what the others in our industry are afraid to do, and we're going to be a force for good in one another's lives and in the lives of our customers.

I envision a time where every Hollywood star is wearing our edible jewelry, where people know the antioxidant count of our dark chocolates and eat them both for pleasure and for health, and when we have sufficient financial resources that allow us to focus on growing our company and ourselves—even if other companies are paralyzed by fear and stress.

So let me try to describe what I see our world at ChocoBot looking like a year from now.

A year from now, there will be absolutely no phone calls into this company griping about broken products. How? We will have eliminated $1 million in operating expense by ensuring that our products arrive at our customers' stores 100% intact. Right now, only 95% of our products arrive intact to our customers. Yes, our products are fragile, but 5% breakage is unacceptable. And frankly, I'm not concerned that we're better than the industry average because I don't think our competitors are pushing that hard on this issue. I mean, really, if we can get 95% there intact, why not the other 5%? So we're going to take a brutal look at the roots of this breakage, whether it's the shipping, the packaging, the chocolate mix, or the number of times we handle the product within the factory. And anybody who has ideas, I want them. No idea is too small or too politically sensitive.

A year from now, you're going to be watching a video of people cheering for a presentation we just made at a national conference about how ChocoBot is making money by saving the environment. How? Specifically, we will have eliminated $1 million in operating expense by going green. I'll be honest; I don't know exactly what we need to do to make that happen. I'm not an expert in green technology. But I know that everyone at this company is very smart and can figure it out. So starting immediately, everyone in the company, in every department, will spend one hour per week learning about green technologies and the ways it can be applied to us. I expect that every department will have a plan with a net savings in excess of $100,000 and that every single employee will have contributed at least one good idea to this effort. Also, we will become so smart in this area that we will be presenting our innovations at a green technology conference next year. You may struggle to use Power-Point, but trust me, in a few months time you'll be able to tell me exactly what an eco-friendly building looks like.

A year from now, people are going to be wearing edible jewelry in the pages of a national fashion magazine. Next year, we'll be taking calls from at least one company on par with Michael Kors or Banana Republic. How? We will have increased sales by $5 million by discovering and inventing unique applications for edible jewelry (this includes developing a partnership with one national organization). Perhaps we can partner with an organization dedicated to reducing high blood pressure or heart disease and use our dark chocolates as a signature piece of jewelry in place of wristbands and ribbons. Remember that dark chocolate is high in antioxidants and studies have found that it can lower blood pressure. Also, I want every employee thinking about the fun, creative ways that you, or people you know, use our products. Maybe it's just a crazy idea you've had, or your brother-in-law's second cousin is the manager for a pop star.

A year from now, a customer is going to send us a letter about how we literally saved him from having to declare personal bankruptcy. How? We will save 15 customers from shutting their doors. This economy has been really hard on us. But it's also been brutal for many of the small businesses (aka specialty candy shops) that sell our products. And the more they suffer, the more we suffer. In our research, we estimate that roughly 30 of these shops are on the verge of closing their doors (we have a list of the ones at risk). We may not be able to save all of them, but we're going to save 15. Over the years, we've developed hundreds of product, marketing, and process innovations in this company, and we're going to collect them all and use them to save 15 of these small businesses. I'm asking every single employee to write down every insight you've had about how to make these shops run more effectively. You've worked with them for years, you know the issues, and you can help save some real businesses and very real people from being victims of this economy. For the next two months, I'm asking every employee to spend up to two hours per week detailing your insights so we can start delivering them to the shops.

I know these goals are not just ambitions; they're hard, and they're going to challenge every single employee of ChocoBot. But we have taken on tough stuff before and come out victorious, and so I have absolute faith in every one of you to achieve the level of greatness—and more—that I set before you today. ChocoBot has earned its fine reputation not only because of our quality products, but also because of the quality of our employees. This coming year will take that reputation to task; if we stay the same, we do nothing more than accept the status quo of being good enough. It's time for all of us to be and do and give more—100 percent more. I don't promise you an easy year, but I do promise you a year filled with innovation, creativity, and substantial reward. In 12 months' time, you will know in your hearts and in your minds that you gave more than you ever thought possible and that other people's lives and livelihoods are better for it—that your individual effort answered a call greater than yourself and you made the world a better place. Let's get to work!

HARD goals are not SMART goals. HARD goals care more about the challenging nature of the goal than about making sure it fits neatly onto a worksheet. HARD goals don't sound formulaic, and that's exactly what makes them so real and so inspiring. When you announce your HARD goals, you're going see visible signs of perspiration and palpations as folks listen. That's what gets the Hundred Percenter adrenaline flowing. Your employees may walk out of the meeting or put down your memo feeling like they just heard a very loud alarm clock. But you can bet every mind is already hard at work coming up with ideas that meet the challenges ahead.

Yet setting and announcing HARD goals isn't all it takes to garner 100% dedication and performance from your team. Our CEO of ChocoBot still has some hard work to do. He will call on a few strategic (and psychological) maneuvers that 100% Leaders rely on to trigger the innate drives and needs for success that exist in each of us. Being a 100% Leader means constantly working to keep employees in the Hundred Percenter zone. It's a tried-and-tested method of basically "pulling" employees with inspiration and motivation and "pushing" them with some illuminating feedback. In other words, Challenge and Connection. It's this dynamic back-and-forth that keeps the tension of HARD goals alive and inspires folks to aspire to Hundred Percenter performance.

The following chapters will share all you need to know to become a 100% Leader who inspires Hundred Percent performance and who makes HARD goals happen.

2

Create Accountability with Constructive Feedback

HARD goals are called HARD goals for a good reason. They *should* challenge even your best people to reach beyond what's tried and tested and comfortable; in other words, the status quo. And like any tough challenge, sometimes before success is reached, folks make mistakes, freeze up, doubt their abilities, or shy away from accountability.

When it comes to HARD goals, errors are inevitable and to be expected, but critical errors left uncorrected are unacceptable. Mistakes left unaddressed are likely to be repeated. This translates to heavy frustration on your part and unnecessary performance limitations on the part of your employees—both of which have no place in a Hundred Percenter workplace.

When mistakes happen, there are typically four ways the situation can go:

1. The mistake is never discussed, or the employee is gently reprimanded. Neither approach makes any impact on the employee's performance whatsoever, and the mistake is soon repeated. (The Appeaser)
2. The employee is scolded unreasonably hard and thus becomes less concerned with improvement and more concerned with vengeance, which creates additional performance problems. (The Intimidator)
3. The mistake is ignored, often with the hope that it will fix itself. (The Avoider)
4. The employee is called on the error and then guided on what can be done to correct and prevent it from happening again, thus inspiring a desire to make a change that results in Hundred Percenter performance. (The 100% Leader)

Those who are 100% Leaders aren't afraid to constructively critique employee performance when warranted. But they understand there's a fine balance between making corrections that do nothing, corrections that push good employees to Hundred Percenter performance, and corrections that either push good employees to stop trying or send them barreling out the door. No one welcomes a humiliating scolding. It makes most people defensive, and once the walls of defensiveness spring up, chances of willing improvement drop into the negative digits.

You may want to say, "Tim, this HARD goal requires strict attention to detail, and your organizational skills are notoriously lousy. If you don't clean up your act, the whole team will suffer because of it." It may be the truth, and probably you and everyone who has known Tim since the first grade knows it, but it won't get Hundred Percenter results. You might hurt Tim's feelings and push him to get his act together—temporarily. But he's probably cursing you under his breath for your insensitive approach and plotting all the ways he can get back at you for making him look like an idiot in public.

It's just as ineffective to use any of the popular softening "tricks," such as "criticize the action, not the person" or "layer the constructive feedback with praise to make it sound kinder and gentler." These techniques don't work, and they have a tendency to backfire and produce results opposite to the ones you want.

The bottom line is that when good people mess up, they get it, and they feel bad about it. They're not racing down the halls, kicking up their heels, and shouting, "Whoopee! I gave our best client misinformation, and he pulled his account!" And if they are, well, you've got a whole different set of problems on your hands.

When good employees make mistakes, whether they are executing HARD goals or going about their day-to-day performance, they usually are aware that things didn't go right. It may be conscious or subconscious, but in most cases, they know on some level they messed up. (Getting people to come to terms with errors and admit them outright may involve a more psychologically sophisticated approach, but we'll get to that in a minute.) The thing to remember is that chances are really good that your best people, when they mess up, have already spent some time sweating out their feelings of lousy self-worth and the repercussions they may face for having made their mistakes. So they don't need you to make them feel bad; they are already doing a really good job of that on their own.

Ultimately, your good performers—your Hundred Percenters and those with the potential to become Hundred Percenters—want to move forward from their mistakes and redeem themselves. What they do need from you is some guidance on why the errors happened, how to correct them, and how to keep them from happening again. And through it all, they want to be treated with respect. After all, these folks have a history of good or promising performance. And mistake or no mistake, that does count for something.

Certainly, 100% Leaders aren't Appeasers who make corrections that send a feel-good message about employee error. No more than they are Intimidators, who send folks running to the restroom in tears over harsh reprimands. Instead, 100% Leaders use a technique called the IDEALS script, which doesn't translate to being a good guy or a bad guy; it's just effective. Look, the whole purpose behind giving constructive feedback is to get the people who made the errors to see and understand the mistakes and care enough not to make them again. Corrective feedback isn't about being nice, and it isn't about being nasty; it's about getting folks to willingly listen and assimilate and to act accordingly.

The IDEALS tool has a great success record with correcting errors and inspiring Hundred Percenter effort. However, the fact remains that the human defense mechanism has been honed over thousands of years, and we the people have developed an impressive array of techniques for avoiding accountability when things go wrong. Before you learn how to approach employees and get them to admit to and correct mistakes, it's imperative to understand the barriers against which you may have to battle on the path to Hundred Percenter performance. Because until you can pull your people up to a place where accountability is possible, you're talking to deaf ears.

When you hear justification for error such as "I never got the memo that said I had to do that," or "I would have had it done if Joe had finished his part of the paperwork," or "I wasn't sure I knew how to use that program, and I was afraid of messing things up," or "I know what I need to do, but there's no way I'll be able to do it all," what you're hearing is Denial, Blame, Excuses, and Anxiety. All very common Stages of Accountability.

Some people accept constructive feedback readily, no matter how it's presented. They take responsibility for whatever they did that was subpar and make the needed changes to do whatever it takes to elevate their future performance. These people are practicing accountability—no excuses, no finger-pointing, no denial, and no freaking out. But most folks aren't quite there yet; they're in one of the lower Stages of Accountability.

We've observed that, besides Accountability, there are four typical reactions to receiving corrective feedback: Denial, Blame, Excuses, and Anxiety. These reactions tend to follow a certain logical flow. For example, Denial begets Blame, which then evolves into Excuses, which is followed by Anxiety. Does everyone evolve through these Stages of Accountability in perfect order? Of course not. People can jump back and forth between the stages. They may never enter Denial, but spend most of their days in Anxiety or Excuses; and they may even have situational-specific reactions (e.g., certain feedback engenders Blame, whereas other feedback is met with Accountability). But as you can see in Figure 2-1, there is a natural logic to the progression of these stages which is useful to understand.

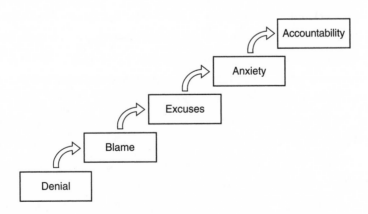

Figure 2-1

The opposite of Accountability tends to be Denial. If you've ever heard people say, "That rule doesn't apply to me" or "My performance was just fine" (even when it wasn't), you've witnessed Denial. These are folks who are so defensive and walled off, or their egos are so fragile, that they're simply not ready for feedback. They're in effect saying, "There's no problem; my performance was absolutely fine. If you don't like the results, that's a problem with your judgment, not my performance."

Once you've pierced the veil of Denial, people often exhibit Blame. Blame is the unspoken acknowledgment that constructive feedback is warranted (i.e., the outcomes were subpar), coupled with an unwillingness to admit any personal fault. You'll hear things like "OK, maybe the results weren't perfect, but go talk to Accounting about why they didn't get the right data to my team before the deadline. You want to know where the problem is, go ask them." Whenever you hear an admission of subpar results followed by somebody else's name (or department), you're hearing Blame. (*Note:* This example presumes you're not in, and don't control, Accounting.)

After Blame comes Excuses. An Excuse is an admission of subpar results plus an admission of fault (insofar as no other person is getting named as the cause of the subpar performance). But a person who makes Excuses isn't quite ready for Accountability. The admission of fault is coupled with a host of extenuating factors that no normal human could possibly have overcome. Unlike Blame, it won't be another person or department that gets thrown under the bus, but your servers, procedures, phone systems, etc. "I didn't get the message," or "The server crashed just as I finished the report," or "We ran out of supplies" are all variations on Excuses.

After Denial, Blame, and Excuses, the final stage before Accountability is often Anxiety. The actual subpar performance and culpability have been fully acknowledged, but the person lacks the readiness to move forward and improve future performance. People in Anxiety say things like "There's no way we'll finish in time" or "We've tried to fix this before, and it just didn't work." These folks get that they're the ones who need to improve, but they lack confidence (they're often freaked out) that they'll be able to make the required improvements.

There's a lot of psychology behind why people try and fall back on Denial, Blame, Excuses, and Anxiety instead of just doing what's asked of them. But you don't need to climb inside your employees' heads to bring them up to Accountability. The 100% Leader shuts down the Denial, Blame, Excuses, and Anxiety with a conversation that we call the IDEALS script—a two-way dialogue focused only on the critical feedback. The IDEALS script works no matter where in the Stages of Accountability employees may be. (After we learn the IDEALS script, we'll return to these Stages of Accountability and tie everything together.)

IDEALS for Delivering Constructive Feedback

Most people get defensive when unchecked and random constructive feedback comes their way. They shoot up invisible walls that block out anything difficult or unpleasant to hear. When this total shutdown happens, it typically pushes people in the opposite direction of Hundred Percenter effort; mistakes go uncorrected and are usually repeated. The 100% Leader follows the IDEALS script, a six-step process that allows constructive feedback to penetrate even the most unwilling of ears and that keeps people motivated during and after the feedback is delivered.

IDEALS stands for:

I. Invite them to partner
D. Disarm yourself
E. Eliminate blame
A. Affirm their control
L. List correct feedback
S. Synchronize your understanding

When applied collectively, the IDEALS technique generates a domino effect that knocks down, and keeps down, the walls of defensiveness. This results in employees who are open to change and who have a clearer picture of how to reach their full Hundred Percenter potential.

Let's take a look at how IDEALS works to keep employees feeling safe, open, and receptive to constructive feedback.

Invite Them to Partner

Katy is the head of nursing for a large teaching hospital. She recently announced a HARD goal to toughen up some personnel issues, one of which was dress code. One member of her team, Jill, is a talented nurse who just misses the mark on reaching her Hundred Percenter potential. For instance, despite Katy's clear presentation of the HARD goal, Jill still comes to work wearing scrubs with the kind of cartoon character prints the HARD goal forbade. This might not be a big deal in a community hospital that has a warm and fuzzy culture, nor would it matter as much if the hospital weren't trying reduce patient confusion by differentiating various types of staff with their colored scrubs. But it definitely doesn't send the right message in this particular teaching hospital, and it definitely defies the HARD goal and Katy's leadership efforts.

If Katy had her way, she'd say something like, "Jill, pull your head out of your posterior and pay attention. I want the behavior to stop. End of discussion." However, aside from the dress code issue, Jill is a good nurse. Katy also knows that while it might feel momentarily good to unload her anger on Jill, it would only make Jill defensive. This would eliminate any chance of solving the problem and helping Jill reach her Hundred Percenter potential. Katy could even lose a potential Hundred Percenter.

The only way Katy will get Jill to change is to approach her nonconfrontationally. She needs to invite Jill to partner in a dialogue. The classic formulation of this invitation goes as follows: "Would you be willing to have a conversation with me about <insert issue here>?"

Katy's invite to Jill can be as simple as, "Jill, would you be willing to have a conversation with me about the new dress code goal?" Katy's invite to partner, directly stated in a sincere and nonthreatening tone, lets Jill know that the meeting isn't going to be a love and praise fest, but that it won't be a yelling and blame session either.

The invitation to partner in dialogue also expresses an openness to hear the other side of the story. This does not mean inviting Jill to give all sorts of excuses. In this particular instance, Jill has been told by more than a few patients that the HARD goal changes to the dress code feel too clinical and depressing. Jill cares about the patients but is too timid to talk to Katy about their feedback. She has been trying to defy orders and please the patients under the guise of excuses. This is all information Katy should be glad to hear.

Let me be clear: I'm not saying that there is always another side to the story. Heck, I'm not even saying there's regularly another side. But every so often, if you view this person as a partner rather than an adversary, you might discover a bit of information that is really going to help you achieve your desired goals.

Face-to-face is the preferable approach to inviting an employee to partner in a dialogue. Not only do the words convey a nonconfrontational situation, but when people hear a relaxed tone and see friendly body language, it enhances their receptivity to the invitation.

In some cases, if the preexisting relationship is strong enough, you can send your invite to partner in a dialogue via e-mail or even text. Younger-generation employees especially love getting text messages from the boss; it shows an effort to communicate using their preferred language. Whatever method you choose to extend the invite, the main thing is to erase all signs of intimidation or fear from your words. You want to send a clear message that this is just two people sitting down to exchange information in order to come to a resolution.

Most people naturally feel safer and perform better when they are given choices, and so you can provide some options about when the talk will take place. This can easily be done by following up your invite with a statement such as, "Do you want to talk now, or would you prefer to wait until after lunch?" While, in theory, you're offering the employee a choice, the catch is that you wrote all the options based upon what you need and want.

Note: There is one caveat to the invitation-to-partner technique. Beware of using the technique if you have a notoriously poor or confrontational relationship with the employee in question and there's a very real possibility he or she will respond, "No, I'm not willing to have a conversation with you." In this case, you want to turn your invite into a statement such as, "We need to have a conversation about <insert issue here>." But be very careful here. You should forgo the invitation format only when a negative relationship exists. Otherwise, you risk damaging a neutral or positive relationship.

Disarm Yourself

Nobody wants to be on the receiving end of hurtful criticism. Granted, you're the boss, and so you have some leverage and leeway. In other words, most employees will let it slide from time to time if you lose your cool and blow up at them. However, if this form of criticism becomes a standard course of action for how you make corrections and instigate change, you're going to push employees, even Hundred Percenters, into reverse motion when it comes to tolerance and performance.

A hurtful criticism from the boss can trigger a chain reaction of work issues the employee may have been shoving under the rug up until now. This can inspire a thought process that goes something like the following: "Fine. I know I messed up the proposal, and it's partly my fault that we lost the client. But did <insert boss's name> have to humiliate me like that? This job just isn't worth it. I'm the only one who pulls my weight around here. I'm stuck working with a bunch of slackers, and the one time I mess up, I get treated like this. I'm definitely getting my résumé out there—today."

If employees suspect that hurtful criticism is going to be part of the experience, they're likely to enter a constructive feedback conversation with some trepidation. This can stop the important message from being heard even before it's delivered. The way 100% Leaders prevent this situation is by making a gesture that says, "No weapons of communication will be used against you in this conversation." This act of openly disarming themselves keeps talented employees feeling safe and open to the critical feedback being delivered.

Christian is a department manager with 25 direct reports. They're a good team, and he tries to be a fair boss, but the unyielding pressure from his own superiors often makes Christian hotheaded and emotional. Soon after the organization announced a HARD goal that demanded greater employee effort and performance, word got out that some members of Christian's team were using company time and computers to send e-mails, update Facebook accounts, and conduct other personal business. Christian's boss, who is not a 100% Leader, gave him an ultimatum to either change the behavior or change jobs.

Christian went back to his department and called an emergency meeting. As the members of his team piled into the conference room, they noticed Christian's face was beet red. His mouth was turned down in an ugly scowl, and his arms were crossed against his chest. "Here it comes again," they all anxiously thought. "Another verbal beating."

And they were right. Christian launched into his attack by basically repeating the Intimidator approach his own boss had used: "You guys are making me look bad again, and I'm sick and tired of it. We're either gonna make some changes in attitude around here, or we're gonna make some changes in staff." His employees' walls of defensiveness shot up in every direction and blocked out everything else Christian had to say. And the Blame, Excuses, Denial, and Anxiety came out in full force.

The situation would have played out differently if Christian had taken a 100% Leader approach to delivering the constructive feedback. He could have started the conversation by openly disarming himself in front of his employees. First, he should have taken some time to cool off after being dressed down by his own boss. Then he could have tried approaching individuals or small groups of team members personally and saying, "There have been some complaints about employees using the Internet for personal use during work hours. Would you be willing to meet as a group to figure out how we can solve this problem? I want everyone to work together to find a comfortable resolution, so I'd like you to bring along any ideas you may have."

In this scenario, Christian disarmed himself by enforcing the fact that this would be a reciprocal conversation. His employees, who are used to his one-sided and hurtful criticisms and who likely resent this behavior a great deal, would certainly take note of the change in his approach. And because Christian personally delivered the invitation in a calm and rational manner, it went the extra mile to show that this wouldn't be another anger session filled with blame and accusations.

Judgment is another verbal weapon that can shut down two-way communication and stand in the way of an effective employee critique. Openly expressing judgment quickly turns a conversation from constructive to destructive and will make employees feel incompetent and discouraged. Disarming yourself of judgment can be done by pausing mid-conversation and saying something like, "I'd like to review the situation to make sure I'm on the same page as you."

If you discover you're on a different wavelength than the employee, you'll need to backtrack and correct the situation. Taking this extra step doesn't mean you're going to necessarily agree with the other party, but it does send a reassuring message that you want to nonjudgmentally understand a perspective other than your own.

When a disconnect between you and an employee does occur, make sure you don't bring judgment into the conversation with statements like:

"You're not making any sense."
"You're not listening to me."

or its shorter cousin:

"Listen to me."

While "You're not making any sense" may sound innocuous at first, it actually points the "you" finger of blame. It implies the other person lacks knowledge and understanding, and it sends a strong message that says, "You're incapable of presenting a clear argument." It is not exactly a message most people will tolerate. The same goes for "You're not listening," which really says, "I don't think you're intelligent enough to understand what I am saying."

None of these are the messages you want to send, which is, "I think you are capable of Hundred Percenter potential."

Instead of saying, "You're not listening to me," assume personal responsibility for the disconnection between the two of you by saying, "I don't think I'm doing a good job of explaining myself." And instead of "You're not making any sense," try saying, "Could you help me understand this issue?" These simple rewrites erase the judgment and accusations and keep the conversation open and fluid. After all, does it really matter who's to blame and why? Isn't the more important issue getting the employee to hear what needs to be said in order to execute a change?

Eliminate Blame

The goal in delivering constructive feedback is not to make employees feel bad for whatever they may have done or thought. As I said earlier, most folks likely already know that they did something wrong, and chances are that they're already suffering for it. Instead of assigning blame, 100% Leaders avoid historical and emotional punishment and focus on solutions. You may not share the same perspectives on situations as your employees do, but you can still work together to develop a plan that moves in a positive direction.

Because of historical evidence, Christian, our leader from the earlier example, has some work to do in order to show his employees that he has no further intention of playing the blame game. One way he can do this is to say in his invite to partner something like, "Look, if we find we have different perspectives, we can discuss that and develop a plan for moving forward." Or if he finds himself in the middle of a conversation with an employee and he sees that a difference of opinion exists, he can interject by saying, "I see we have very different opinions on this. That's fine. But let's work together to find a resolution."

Affirm Their Control

In order to keep people fully engaged in a conversation that involves constructive feedback, it's important to reaffirm that they have some control over the situation. Recognizing the importance of this, 100% Leaders check in on a regular basis by saying, "Does that sound OK?"

This simple question reminds employees that they have a say in the matter and that you care about how they are doing and what they are thinking. In Christian's case, this tactic would resolve much of the Denial, Blame, Excuses, and Anxiety his people are probably feeling. It would show that Christian is in fact listening and that he cares, reaffirming the sincerity of his invite to partner in dialogue.

As an added bonus, affirming the other party's control is a quick check of whether he or she remains receptive to your words. If the answer is, "No, that doesn't sound OK to me," or you get a rapid-fire list of defensive questions in response, you can be pretty sure the conversation is off track. Again, you need to backtrack and fix this situation before you move on.

List Correct Feedback

When 100% Leaders deliver constructive feedback, they take nothing for granted. It's not that they doubt their employees' intelligence or feel the need to hypermanage them. They simply recognize that it doesn't hurt to take the extra effort to make a crystal clear statement that details exact expectations.

The golden rule for giving constructive feedback is that the feedback:

Makes perfect sense
Holds up to logical scrutiny

Is understandable

Teaches sufficiently

The following two techniques will make sure you hit every factor of the golden rule.

Don't Skimp on the Details

No matter how small a detail may be, if it's something employees are going to be held accountable for, make sure you give them the information they need. This is especially important when delivering HARD goals. A lot of leaders worry that giving minutely detailed constructive feedback makes them come off like a control freak or a micromanager. Admirably, they take conscious steps to temper their words and refrain from harping on the intimate details of how they want something done.

Granted, no one wants to work under a micromanager. And certainly, employees who feel they have the trust and confidence of the boss more often than not remain happily engaged in their work. But when clarity is sacrificed as part of the preventative, no one wins.

There's a simple principle that establishes the dividing line between what constitutes micromanagement and constructive feedback:

If something is *not* optional and if you *will* hold the employees accountable if they don't do it, you *must* give clear and logical feedback.

Nothing kills employee morale faster than when the boss withholds critical information and then admonishes employees when results fail to meet expectations. This happens in countless cases where the boss doesn't even realize he or she has failed to provide clear directions. Protect yourself and your employees from this situation by never assuming there is a thorough understanding of anything for which employees can be punished or fired.

Explain Why

One critical aspect of giving constructive feedback that most leaders miss is letting employees know *why* they're being asked to do something. This is often the factor that makes or breaks what employees do, how well they do it, and how happy they are doing it.

It's critical to note that if you abuse the power of *why*, you risk losing the effectiveness behind the why. If you really don't have a good reason why you want something done a certain way, don't make the correction. Let some things be negotiable. Then, when a situation comes up where you really can't offer a why, whether due to confidentiality, the pressure of time, or some arbitrary rule from on high, you'll still have the trust and cooperation of your best people.

It's always a good idea to follow up constructive feedback in writing, including the why. Unless your employees have total recall, and unfortunately for leaders, few of them do, some important detail is almost guaranteed to get lost. Putting it in writing also provides a visual aid, and that's important in today's world of seemingly endless auditory, visual, and sensory stimulation. Finally, when you've got it in writing, there can be no disputing what was said.

Synchronize Your Understanding

This final step is where the partnership aspect of the dialogue kicks in. Granted, if you're forced to correct an employee error, you likely already know the outcome you want. Usually it's for the employee to replace the undesirable behavior with an effort you define as Hundred Percenter. But you'll never win an employee's buy-in to change if you tell the employee to shut up and follow orders.

When you ask an employee, "Tell me how you think we can work together to build on this and make things even more effective next time," there's no overbearing rank being pulled. There's also no recrimination for the behavior you've called into question. It's just an invite to work together and to make things better.

And because it's an open-ended question, with no presumed answer, it encourages discussion. If you were to simply ask, "Do you understand my feedback?" it's possible to come off sounding condescending; an approach that is guaranteed to raise defensiveness and shut down effectiveness. And since a question like that isn't likely to produce more than a yes-or-no answer, you also lose the litmus test of the employee's understanding of the feedback.

BTW: Constructive Feedback Is Different from Advice

One mistake a lot of leaders make is delivering advice instead of constructive feedback. This only confuses the matter, raises the other party's defensiveness, and pushes the person in the opposite direction of Hundred Percenter performance. You may think it's nicer to phrase criticisms more gently by injecting words like "should," "would," "ought," "gotta, "must," and "try." The problem is that by using these words, your constructive feedback becomes advice:

> Personally, I wouldn't bother the client before noon.
> If it were me, I'd get started on this right away.
> Have you tried talking to the client?
> You should probably make a few extra just in case.

There's no language in any of the above statements that indicates that the "would," "should," etc., is mandatory. If it's not optional, then don't imply it is. Trying to trick employees into thinking they have a choice when they really don't doesn't make the work any more enjoyable. And if they interpret your feedback as optional and do it their way (the non–Hundred Percenter way) and it turns out wrong, everyone suffers.

There are five core reasons why advice negates the effectiveness of constructive feedback and raises defensiveness. Let's take a look.

Why Advice Doesn't Work Reason #1: Judgment

When you give unasked-for advice, it sends an underlying and very judgmental message of "You're obviously not as savvy as I am, because if you were, you'd have already figured out what I'm telling you." You may not consciously intend to promote this message, but it's usually what the person on the receiving end of advice hears. And it won't inspire anyone to become a Hundred Percenter.

What's more, if you continually offer unsolicited advice, there's a good chance people will retaliate and let you know, in no uncertain terms, about your own faults. You may think you're being helpful, or you may truly believe you know better, but you won't convince anyone who's stuck listening to your advice. The person on the other side of your endless stream of "You should . . . " and "You better . . . " is probably thinking, "Who the heck is this bozo to be giving me advice? He should clean up his own mess and then come talk to me."

Why Advice Doesn't Work Reason #2: Directive

When you give advice, in essence you're telling somebody else what to do. This implies that you have all the answers about what works and what doesn't. But how could you? Chances are you don't have all the background information on the situation, nor do you understand the other person's emotions and motivations.

There's absolutely no constructive value in statements like "Well, if it were me, I would . . . " It's not you, and hearing this kind of advice only puts the other party on red alert that it may be time to check out of the conversation. You asked the employee to partner in dialogue, so allow that person to provide additional facts about the situation. Or if the employee has nothing to voluntarily offer, ask a few questions that prompt responses to fill in the blanks. But be careful. Sometimes the questions we ask are no more than a thinly disguised form of unsolicited advice.

I had a recent experience where my laptop froze while I was at a client site. The client called in his tech support department, and the first thing one of the IT guys asked me was "Did you try rebooting it?" Now, that may be the question everybody asks, but it's not a question that indicates that the person asking it sees the other person as intelligent or a Hundred Percenter. Instead, it's a directive, a form of speaking down, and it comes off sounding strongly like advice.

Here's the internal reaction I had to his "advice" question: <Sarcastically> "Holy crap, you mean you can restart a laptop? Why didn't I think of that? I mean, every day I turn it *on*, but I never thought about turning it *off*. They clearly don't pay you enough because that is absolute *genius*!"

Of course, I bit my tongue and answered his question. But what if he'd instead asked me, "What actions have you taken so far?" There's a big difference between that latter question and "Did you try rebooting it?" The latter acknowledges that you consider the other person's input and intelligence as something valuable. It's also a legitimate attempt to gather information. The former, as we have said, is unsolicited advice.

When It's OK to Be Directive. We don't mean to imply you should never be directive. When you're a superior telling a subordinate what to do, it's perfectly acceptable. But even in that situation, you still need to be careful that you're giving directions—not advice.

Because if you give advice, you're only setting the stage for a terrible dynamic.

Here's an example of what we mean:

Scenario: The boss sees the employee writing a report.

BOSS: I wouldn't use those colors for that report. I'd go with something brighter.
EMPLOYEE: Sure, OK.

Later that day, the employee finishes the report and presents it to the boss.

BOSS: What the heck is this? I told you to use brighter colors.
EMPLOYEE: No, you said *you* would use something brighter. I liked the colors I was already using just fine.
BOSS: Listen, when I tell you to do something, I just want you to do it.
EMPLOYEE: Then next time tell me what you want.

As a superior, you have the right (and obligation) to give directions and make corrections. However, when you phrase it as advice, it sounds more like a recommendation than a directive. And as we've seen, that creates a misunderstanding that wastes everyone's time.

To avoid these kinds of situations, follow the rule from the "Don't Skimp on the Details" section above: if what you need to tell a subordinate is *not* optional, then be honest with the person. Don't play coy and pretend the person has a choice when actually he or she doesn't.

Why Advice Doesn't Work Reason #3: Inflexibility
When you give advice, you offer the other party only two choices: take the advice, or ignore the advice. If your advice is taken, that

means the other person must tacitly admit you're right and he or she is wrong. This automatically gives you credit for being smarter. This is a dangerous scenario, and it's one that's almost guaranteed to create defensiveness.

When advice is ignored, it invites the possibility of an "I told you so." And that can prompt our old friend, the walls of defensiveness, to spring up and block out the feedback. Even if you outwardly don't acknowledge the failure to take your advice, the person who passed on taking it may fear you're insulted. This scenario can shut down the employee from attempting any future discussion on the topic (or any other topic for that matter). And then there's always the chance that your constant advice and inflexibility has you positioned as someone to be avoided.

Why Advice Doesn't Work Reason #4: Narcissism

Let's be honest. Sometimes we give advice because we want to demonstrate how smart we are or because we feel left out or need to be needed. There are even cases where constructive feedback is manipulated to vent anger or to purposely hurt someone. But it's always done under the thinly veiled guise of trying to be helpful.

Before you offer constructive feedback, consider your reasons. If your purpose is not to help someone reach Hundred Percenter effort, you probably want to rethink giving the feedback.

Why Advice Doesn't Work Reason #5: Unsolicited

Most advice is offered unsolicited. This means the other party didn't ask to be judged, corrected, or directed. When you catch people off guard and hit them upside the head with advice, there's virtually no chance they'll be in an open emotional state to hear what you say.

Putting It All Together

To sum up the IDEALS technique, here's a quick review of the strategies and a simple script for each:

I.   Invite the person to partner: "Would you be willing to have a conversation with me about X, Y, Z? Does right now work, or would you rather wait until after lunch?"

D.   Disarm yourself: "I'd like to review the situation to make sure I'm on the same page as you."

E.   Eliminate blame: "And if we have different perspectives, we can discuss those and develop a plan for moving forward."

A.   Affirm their control: "Does that sound OK to you?"

L.   List correct feedback: "The behavior I am seeing is X, Y, Z, and what I need to see is A, B, C."

S.   Synchronize your understanding: "Tell me how you think we can work together to build on this and make things even more effective next time."

Imagine the following situation: You're launching a new ad campaign, and you give a HARD goal that puts Joe, a potential Hundred Percenter, in charge of finalizing the itinerary for an important client meeting. Despite the fact that you've seen several drafts of the itinerary, Joe shows up to the meeting empty-handed.

You're pretty angry about this because it leaves you looking unprepared and amateurish in front of the client. You pull through the meeting and then approach Joe to discuss what happened. Below are two options for starting your conversation:

Version A: "I gotta tell you, Joe, I'm pretty ticked about not having the itinerary. You obviously didn't listen when I said you were in charge of getting it done. Your irresponsibility made me look like a total fool. If you want to sabotage your career, that's fine, but don't screw up my career too. If you're not going to do something, just tell me so I can do it myself like everything else."

Version B: "Joe, would you be willing to have a conversation with me about the missing itinerary? I'd like to review the situation to make sure I'm on the same page as you. And if we have a different perspective, which is totally possible, we'll work that out and come up with a plan for the future. Does that sound OK? Great. Do you have time now, or do you want to wait until after lunch?"

Which version is likely to make Joe receptive to the message you need to deliver about his performance? And which version is sending Joe the message that he's under attack and that he needs to raise his guard? The situation isn't going to get remedied until Joe changes his behavior, and you need his willing participation to make that happen.

It's clear that Version B is the choice a 100% Leader would make.

Here's the one comeback that some leaders have to Version B: "But I'm really ticked at Joe, and he needs to know that. He let me down, and I feel betrayed. Version B makes it sound like I'm letting his behavior slide, and I can't allow that."

That's a very legitimate response. We've all felt those same thoughts, and we've all had that same emotional itch to be scratched. But here's the problem: Joe is a talented employee, and we want to hold on to him while we help him improve his behavior and improve his performance. And the question is whether making Joe defensive is the best way to accomplish that.

Version A is virtually guaranteed to make Joe defensive. And if his defensiveness makes him aggressive, you're going to have a fight on your hands. And if he becomes passive, he'll endure your emotional browbeating, but he may subtly sabotage you down the road.

Tweaking the IDEALS Script

I began this chapter by outlining the Stages of Accountability (Denial, Blame, Excuses, Anxiety, and Accountability). I then took you through the IDEALS script, designed to deliver critical feedback no matter what Stage of Accountability an employee is in. Now, I'm going to offer one more tweak and combine both the Stages of Accountability and the IDEALS script.

For many leaders, the $64,000 question is, "What do I actually say when I hear Denial, Blame, Excuses, and Anxiety, especially right before or after I've delivered the IDEALS script?" We designed the IDEALS script to work in every one of these stages. But you may do a little tweaking in how you deliver, or repeat, the IDEALS script depending on which stage the employee currently inhabits.

Denial

Denial is often the most frustrating stage of employee accountability a leader can face. When confronted with a person who just doesn't "get it," there's a natural tendency to want to reach across the desk and throttle that person. There's another, and similarly ineffective, reaction some leaders have, which is to soften the feedback. This typically involves throwing a compliment in with the correction to try and make folks feel less defensive. (This "Compliment Sandwich" technique may be one of the worst management techniques ever created, and for more on why it's so bad, see Chapter 3, "Reclaiming Our Heroes with Positive Reinforcement.")

When confronted with Denial, you want to remain candid, but in a very calm and matter-of-fact way. You can't punch your way through a wall of defensiveness. Yelling and screaming just doesn't work. Hyperbole (i.e., exaggerating or "amping up" the seriousness of the issue at hand) is just as ineffective. Stick to your facts. Keep the conversation as specific, calm, and data-driven as you can. If you've completed the IDEALS script, but the employee is still in Denial, go back and do it again with special emphasis on L: List corrective feedback.

Don't let yourself become an Intimidator, Appeaser, or Avoider. Just repeat the script. A technique that psychologists call the broken record technique (for obvious reasons) is an incredibly powerful tool for penetrating the walls of defensiveness. You don't have to keep repeating the I, D, E, and A parts, but one or two more times through the L will usually do the trick.

Blame

When you give corrective feedback to someone in the Blame stage, you're likely to hear a reaction such as, "Well, I could maybe fix my part, but nothing's going to work until we fix Accounting." The party that gets blamed will typically be one outside your control, which is an attempt to deflate, or completely deter, any corrective action you intended to take.

The first time this happens is the signal that you need to actively redirect the focus of your conversation. Simply say, "All I want to focus on right now is what we can control." Of course, the employee will likely retort, "But Accounting is the real problem here," to which you will reply, "Accounting is not my concern. I want to discuss those issues that are under our control, right here, right now." As you might do in the Denial stage, you may have to repeat yourself a few times. But remember, there can be no conversation about blaming Accounting if you absolutely refuse to entertain the conversation.

Excuses

Excuses are very easy to fix. They are motivated by a fear of being blamed, so all you have to do is remove the presumption of blame, and excuses generally go away. Years ago, I destroyed my car. Through a combination of abusive driving and lack of attention to certain warnings, I basically blew up the engine. The car died while I was on a highway. I had to get towed 100 miles, and it cost me thousands of dollars to fix.

When I walked in the door that night and explained everything to my wife, I had a list of world-class excuses ready to go. After all, I deserved blame; I was totally at fault for both killing my car and for being a total moron. But my wife looked at me and said, "So when do you pick up your car?" I don't want to infer that she was happy. She clearly understood I was a moron, but she analyzed the situation and saw that blame wasn't going to get the car back any faster, nor was it going to teach me any more lessons than I had already taught myself. (It does help that I'm married to an A-list clinical psychologist with the patience of Job.)

I didn't need my excuses because I wasn't being blamed (I wasn't being excused, but I wasn't being blamed). My wife did monitor my car maintenance for a while (she even got creative with Family Car Day, where we both take our cars in for servicing and then go out to a fun breakfast with the kids), and today my car could star in commercials for a 50-point Jiffy Lube check.

When you hear lots of excuses from your employees, it means they're under the impression that you're blaming them or about to blame them (you may not actually be doing any blaming, but that's what they've internalized). The simple resolve is to say, "I'm not interested in fixing any blame; I'm only interested in fixing the problem."

Does this mean you excuse the behavior? Of course not. You're still going to track mistakes and failures, and too many may result in poor reviews, action plans, and even dismissal. But the moment you hear an excuse, your concern has to be fixing the issue. If you've got a project on deadline that needs to get out the door ASAP, you can do your employee write-up 15 minutes later. It's far more critical to act immediately to fix the problem and deliver the project.

Anxiety

When you hear Anxiety, you've got a person who is on the verge of Accountability. The employee understands his or her culpability and even understands the solution, but that person is overwhelmed by what comes next. In these cases, take your corrective feedback, and break it into bite-size chunks.

Anxious people need process steps (Step 1 we do this, then Step 2 we do this, etc.). Does it take a few extra minutes? Sure, but what are your options? If you let people wallow in their anxiety, they're not going to take care of the problem or change the behavior. So take your corrective feedback, break it up, and get them started. You should also plan to do more frequent checking-in. Touch base after the first step to make any necessary corrections, then after the second step, etc. Usually after the first two steps, anxiety will be lowered, the employee will be in a groove, and you'll probably see someone who's successfully entered full Accountability.

Just remember: employees need corrective feedback, they know they need it, and they actually want it. The IDEALS script is a way to ensure employees don't spend their emotional energy denying, blaming, excusing, or being anxious about the performance in need of correction. Denial, Blame, Excuses, and Anxiety are natural, and fairly common, reactions to critical feedback. If you use the IDEALS script, with the adaptations mentioned above, you will lower people's walls of defensiveness, they'll absorb your feedback, and you'll be looking at Hundred Percenters.

3

Reclaim Our Heroes with Positive Reinforcement

Here's a shocking finding: when we asked more than 5,000 employees to tell us who teaches them more about the dos and don'ts on the job, the boss or fellow employees, 67% said they learn more by watching fellow employees.

This should make you wonder: what do your employees learn about being a Hundred Percenter from watching their coworkers? Let me offer two very bad lessons that the typical employee is learning every single day.

Lesson #1: Being a Hundred Percenter Stinks

Imagine it's Friday afternoon at 4 p.m. and you've got a major report due on Monday at 9 a.m. This report could derail your career if it's not done right, and you're going to need some help getting it done. It's going to be a tough weekend of hard work, but a deadline is a deadline. Whom are you going to turn to for help: the employee who gives 100% effort or the employee who gives 50% effort? Of course, you take the Hundred Percenter. When the same situation happens again next week, who do you think gets called on to make the painful sacrifice? The Hundred Percenter. And it's the Hundred Percenter who will get the call the weekend after that and the weekend after that.

Now, answer this question: who has the worst job in your department? Say it with me: the Hundred Percenter. There are two morals here: First, create more Hundred Percenters (just follow all the rules in this book). Second, when your non–Hundred Percenters are looking at your Hundred Percenters, they're probably not learning the lesson that you hope they are. Instead, they're likely learning that being a Hundred Percenter is hard and painful, a lesson that results in saying, "No thank you to that job!"

Lesson #2: The Boss Can't Tell the Difference Between Hundred Percenters and Fifty Percenters

Imagine you've got two employees who just finished meeting a deadline for a very tough project. Chris is a Hundred Percenter, and he did an incredible job (while giving 100%, of course). Pat is a Fifty Percenter who did a passable job (no glaring mistakes, just not nearly as good a job as the Hundred Percenter). Now, they're both standing in front of you waiting for some feedback. Here's what the typical manager says, "Chris and Pat, thanks for getting this done on time, good work."

What did they learn? Pat learned that giving 50% and doing passable work is totally fine. Pat's thinking, "Heck, giving 100% must be for chumps if we both just got the same feedback." Chris learned that giving 100% doesn't get noticed, and Chris's thoughts will sound like "How many more times am I going to give 100% when the boss seems to think that 50% is every bit as good as 100%?"

Why Are We Teaching These Terrible Lessons?

It's easy to dump everything on our Hundred Percenters because they're, well, Hundred Percenters. And in the short term, developing more Hundred Percenters to spread the load seems like more work than just abusing the few we've already got. Yes, the bill will come due when those Hundred Percenters quit, but as we've seen in other chapters, for many folks, denial ain't just a river in Egypt.

We also do a lousy job of distinguishing between Hundred Percenters and everyone else. Largely, this is because of the mothering we got as children. Comments such as "Don't make Pat feel bad," or "Don't play favorites," or "Doing well is its own reward" were common refrains. It's easy to let our compensation systems differentiate Hundred Percenters (assuming your compensation systems actually do that), but it's a lot harder to differentiate the Hundred Percenter crowd when we've got the whole department standing around looking at us.

Of course, we're not allowed to play favorites on the basis of race, age, religion, sex, sexual preference, health status, and all the rest. But we are allowed to play favorites on the basis of performance (or effort or teamwork or grit or anything controllable and job related). If I'm Phil Jackson coaching the 1996 Chicago Bulls, I'm allowed to have a favorite player (Michael Jordan). I'm allowed to have a second favorite player (Scottie Pippen). I'm allowed to have third favorite players (anybody who gets those two guys the ball). There's no law that says I have to give equal praise to people who don't play their position or who miss their shots.

Not only are leaders allowed to differentiate your Hundred Percenters, but they're also required to do so. Across our employee survey database, comprising hundreds of thousands of employee survey respondents, over 70% of people say that Hundred Percenters should receive more rewards and recognition than others.

The challenge we've got is twofold: we've got to keep our Hundred Percenters continually striving to give 100%, *and* we've got to teach everyone else how and why to become a Hundred Percenter. In the sections that follow, I'm going to show you, first, how to recognize your Hundred Percenters and keep them motivated— without throwing money at them. Second, I'm going to show you how to use a related technique to teach and motivate everyone else to become a Hundred Percenter.

Ending Our Reliance on Money

"I would love to have even one Hundred Percenter," said Joe, who heads the claims processing department of a large insurance company. "I'm in charge of 30 people, and while the work isn't brain surgery, it is target oriented." Joe estimates his team is primarily made of Fifty to Seventy-Five Percenters, in other words, satisficers. "They get the work done okay," says Joe, "but we're rarely on schedule, and that affects a lot of people. Some days I feel like the most hated guy on the planet."

When Joe was asked how he motivates his team, his frustration grew. "My hands are tied when it comes to financial incentives. The company does the yearly review thing along with standard percentage raises. So nobody's getting stoked over that. I do what I can, birthdays with the cake and balloons, anything to inspire a sense of team. Look, we push paper around in my department. It's far from exciting. Without money, there's no real motivation for anyone to do anything."

Joe, like a lot of leaders, believes money is what inspires employees to give above-and-beyond performance. However, if you ask your Hundred Percenters what it is that pushes them to give more than their lower-performing peers, most of them are going to list a lot of things before they get to money. Hundred Percenters appreciate money, but more than that, they are after an emotional charge that comes from being recognized for who they are. And unless it's their passion, they don't need to be saving the manatees or feeding a third world country in order to get satisfaction. They just want to know that what they contribute on a day-to-day basis makes a difference.

"Oh, you're talking about praise," Joe responds. "I know all about praise. I read all the books, and that's exactly how I raised my son. And you know what he turned into? He's one of those Gen Yers you hear about. All that praise went right to his head. He thinks that he can do no wrong and that the world is there to provide just for him. I've seen what praise can do, and it's not for me. This is work, not Disneyland. If people want to get warm fuzzies just for showing up every day, they're in the wrong place."

Once again, Joe is making a common mistake—one that keeps a lot of would-be Hundred Percenters firmly rooted in satisficing. And it's easy to understand why so many leaders make this error. The blame absolutely belongs to "Praise early, praise often," what up until the present day has largely been the mantra of our times. Joe's right; the world, and especially our country, got too soft, things got too easy, and a lot of people got put on a pedestal for doing absolutely nothing special.

But there's a shift going on in the world—and in this country. There is a cry for change, and it applies to our government, our homes, and our workplaces. It's time to reclaim a culture that honors a genuine work ethic and to push ourselves to greatness again. But that doesn't mean throwing the baby out with the bathwater. We still need to commend the folks who go above and beyond— that is, if we want them to keep giving Hundred Percenter effort.

Positive Reinforcement Instead of Praise

Positive reinforcement is not praise, and it's not warm and fuzzy. It's a teaching tool that addresses a well-documented psychological principle that says that desirable behavior—when reinforced— gets repeated. Leaders who communicate a clear message that says, "The thing you just did right there; that way . . . it's good. Do more of it," deliver positive feedback that increases the frequency and intensity of Hundred Percenter behavior. These are the leaders who keep their Hundred Percenters on track and make a good many of their non–Hundred Percenters hungry for the same.

One of our studies found that bosses who give significant positive recognition to Hundred Percenters get 270% more buy-in when they assign HARD goals. And yet 61% of employees say their boss does a lousy job of recognizing and acknowledging their accomplishments. Take Marilynne, for instance, who works in retail and who went out of her way to help a customer obtain the out-of-stock items he needed. When the customer wrote a letter to the store commending Marilynne's performance, her boss merely shoved the letter in with her paycheck. He never said a word about it.

When we asked leaders why they hold back from giving deserved positive reinforcement, the overwhelming response was

"I don't do positive reinforcement, even with my top talent. It just feels too much like praise."

But then there are leaders like Frank. When Adrienne, one of his organization's paralegals, noticed that some of the client files were missing important contracts and other legal documents, she quickly brought it to his attention. Together, they conducted a panicked survey of the organization's filing system. They discovered the secretary in charge of filing, who had walked off the job a week earlier, had been filing things wherever she could shove them, just to get the job done. Contracts for one client were in another client's file, and there was a huge fear that some contracts may have gone missing entirely. Obviously, this put the organization in a great deal of potential legal peril.

Adrienne volunteered to overhaul the filing system, even if it meant late hours and some weekends. As she sorted through the mess, she recognized that even where things were filed correctly, the whole system was outdated and inefficient. She put together a mock-up of an improved sample file and showed it to Frank. He loved the idea and asked her to implement the system. He even hired a temp to assist her in the job. It took a few weeks, but finally every missing contract and legal document had been accounted for and reordered.

Frank recognized that Adrienne's commitment to seeing the job through, and her incentive to not just do what she was asked, but more, was the Hundred Percenter attitude he wanted on his team. In addition to thanking Adrienne, he threw a department lunch in her honor. It wasn't much, but it made Adrienne feel a bit like a celebrity, like she had done something important. Frank also called Adrienne into his office to discuss her future with the company, including some special projects she might want to be part of.

Adrienne, who had actually been thinking of checking out of the job and going to law school, suddenly felt less inspired to leave.

She was attracted to hard work, which was what had made law school so appealing. She also liked being appreciated for her efforts. She'd never had a boss like Frank, and certainly no one had given her a temp or a lunch or had offered her extra projects just for doing what she loved to do. Five years after the fact, Adrienne is still happily working for the same company. Her Hundred Percenter attitude has brought a continual positive effect to her work and to those around her. Once in a while she jokes about law school and how it was just a dream she had before she found a job, and a boss, that fulfilled her.

Most leaders wait until something goes wrong before they even think about giving employee feedback. And then it's only negative. Negative reinforcement can work to cease unwanted behavior, but it does nothing to optimize performance, nor is it nearly as powerful a teaching tool as positive reinforcement. As anyone who has been on the receiving end of negative reinforcement knows, the responding motivation is to figure out the best way to avoid getting "yelled at" again. Negative reinforcement might work to stop an employee's undesirable behavior, but there's no guarantee that the behavior that replaces it will be even close to what you want. All of this means it's time to stop waiting for things to go wrong and start noticing—and commenting—when things go right.

The Four Components of Positive Reinforcement

Whether it's a Hundred Percenter whom you want to keep that way or whether you're trying to push the buttons that will transform a satisficer into a Hundred Percenter, there are four components you definitely want to hit when delivering positive feedback:

Make it meaningful.

Be specific.

Make it timely: catch 'em in the act.

Keep it free of criticism.

Let's take a closer look at how positive reinforcement works—and how you can make it work for you.

Make It Meaningful

You don't need to blow constant smoke to make and maintain Hundred Percenters. In fact, doling out meaningless praise is guaranteed to work against you. Hundred Percenters are never happy when rewards are vague or distributed on a widespread level. It provides no learning curve and no differentiation that their performance stands out from everyone else's.

Say you tell Mary, who always gives 100%, "Great job" whenever she deserves it. But you also tell Bob, who on a good day maybe gives 75%, the same exact thing when he manages to slide by with acceptable results. What Bob is going to hear is that by giving 75%, he's just as good as Mary. And that's not going to inspire him to work any harder and become a Hundred Percenter. As for Mary, all she's hearing is that her 100% is no better than satisficing. From this, Mary will think, "Why bother giving 100% when 75% gets me the same reward." Which means either Mary will get ticked off and start to slack or she will start to doubt her abilities and lose her Hundred Percenter edge.

The only folks who appreciate empty praise are low performers. Hundred Percenters want meaningful feedback. One leader, Tom, found this out the hard way. He was in the midst of executing a massive mailing that, due to budget cuts, was being done in-house. He set an employee, Madison, to work stuffing envelopes.

Anxious to keep her working at as high a level as possible, Tom called Madison in to his office at the end of the first day to give her a little psychological boost. In the past, Madison had shown signs of being a Hundred Percenter, and Tom wanted to keep her motivated and energized and moving forward toward that aim.

"I'm really impressed with your efforts today," Tom said. "Your work on this mailing project is really terrific." Then he sat back and waited for a sign that the positive reinforcement had registered. He was expecting a big smile or some gushing thanks.

When all Madison did was look at him like he had 12 heads, Tom asked her what was on her mind. "You're kidding, right?" Madison said.

Tom replied, "No, I really wanted you to know what a great job you are doing."

Madison fidgeted uncomfortably for a few minutes and then, in a timid voice, said, "This is really hard for me to say to my boss, but I know if I don't say something, I am going to walk away from here regretting it. Look, I'm stuffing envelopes right now. I mean, I know it has to get done and I don't mind doing it, but I have done some pretty remarkable things on the job, and it wasn't stuffing envelopes. It makes me feel like all you think I'm good at are menial tasks."

Tom learned a valuable lesson that day. Empty praise holds no value with Hundred Percenters or even potential Hundred Percenters. Complimenting these folks for unchallenging tasks, or work they didn't actually do, is counterproductive. Not only does it kill their desire to work harder, but it also diminishes their trust in you as a leader.

Be Specific

Daniel, the director of a small community hospital, is a great believer in the power of praise. He always tries to compliment his team on the good work he sees taking place. It's not uncommon for employees to get a "Looking good," "Keep up the great work," or "That's what I like to see," as Daniel passes by. But despite his good intentions, Daniel's words are too vague to deliver any message of real value. The only thing he inspires from his team are snickers at his meaningless and predicable words.

"Great job" doesn't qualify as positive reinforcement. It's empty praise, and it delivers a zero learning curve. Which means the person on the receiving end, especially a Hundred Percenter, will probably take it in one ear and send it out the other. In order to be effective, positive feedback must provide a clear picture of the specific performance that's being commended.

It may seem as if "great job" goes up a notch if you tack on something like, "I like your attention to detail." But that still doesn't specify what details about the behavior you actually liked and want to see again. If you want employees to repeat the performance, you've got to tell them exactly what they did right.

Once Daniel learned the importance of being specific, he changed his approach to giving out positive reinforcement. Instead of buzzing around and handing out vague compliments, he now comes to a full stop in front of the employee he wishes to address. Sometimes he even calls the employee into his office for a one-on-one chat. Once he has the employee's full attention, he paints a picture of the work he wants to commend by saying something like, "Aaron, the way you got Mr. X's tests done ahead of schedule means a lot to both me and Mr. X. And the updated format you suggested to record the results looks really promising. I want to schedule a time to explore that further with you, and I hope you keep bringing me new ideas."

Now Aaron has a lot to think about. For example, he might think: "You know, I did do a good job with Mr. X. I had to give up my lunch and really hustle to get those lab results in on time, but it sure was worth it. It felt really good to have Daniel take notice of my efforts like that. I wasn't sure about the new format, but I guess it was a good idea. I wonder what else I can do to make things better around here."

When positive reinforcement provides a visualization of the specific skills and abilities that constitute desirable high performance, it gives people something to grab on to and run with. It keeps current Hundred Percenters firmly on track of what makes the best, and it gives those who have the potential to be Hundred Percenters clear guidelines about what constitutes a Hundred Percenter measurement of success.

As an added benefit, anyone who witnesses the positive reinforcement, such as any employees who heard Daniel talking to Aaron, is going to be inspired to give a little more to try and get the same. Positive reinforcement is infectious.

Make It Timely: Catch 'Em in the Act

Positive reinforcement depends on a brain connection that associates the reward with the desired behavior. So asking employees (and especially Hundred Percenters) to wait a year for some constructive feedback is like asking them to wait an eternity. If you want positive feedback to carry full impact, it has to be delivered in real time.

Once again, this doesn't mean wandering about the workplace offering meaningless praise. It does mean looking for teachable moments and giving supportive documentation as they're happening. When Aaron had the test results done early, Daniel was right there to say, "Hey. You got this done ahead of schedule, and that's terrific." Think about the impact of that message 6, 8, or 12 months after the fact. If Daniel even remembered to include it in a yearly review, it would likely leave Aaron scratching his head and wondering, "What test results? Mr. X, who?"

Keep It Free of Criticism

There's a definite place and time for constructive feedback, and it most definitely is *not* when you're delivering a positive message. Too many leaders make the mistake of trying to squeeze a negative performance critique or correction between layers of positive reinforcement. This is called the Compliment Sandwich, and it doesn't work. It's like trying to tell your kid to get off drugs while praising him or her for mowing the lawn last Saturday. It's a crazy mixed message that gets zero results.

Joanne was having trouble motivating one of her employees, Ashley, to more closely follow company policy regarding customer service. There were a lot of things about Ashley's performance that were outstanding, close to Hundred Percenter, and so Joanne didn't want to chase her away with negative feedback. She decided the best method was to soften the criticism by lacing it in with a few compliments. That way she figured she could help Ashley correct her mistakes while still reinforcing her strengths that were a value to the company.

She pulled Ashley aside and said, "I wanted to tell you what a great job you did dealing with that difficult customer last week. Even though she was visibly upset, you kept your cool and helped her resolve the problem. Satisfied customers are what we are here to create. I did notice you arguing with another customer this afternoon though, and that isn't so good. But again, last week, you were right on target."

Ashley returned to the selling floor, and Joanne was hopeful that her message had been received. Her goal had been to soften the blow of the criticism with the good feeling that comes with positive reinforcement, but to still let Ashley know she needed to improve. Ashley's coworkers were on her in an instant, curious about what had just gone down with Joanne. "Oh, it was nothing bad," Ashley told them. "Remember that crazy customer I had last week? I guess Joanne is happy I didn't flip out on her or anything. I don't know. I'm not really sure what she wanted. I guess she was just trying to tell me I'm doing a good job."

Joanne struck out on both counts by using a Compliment Sandwich. Her positive message was received, but it was clouded by the negative feedback layered in the middle. As for the constructive criticism, it wasn't heard at all. If anything, Ashley got a slight boost that her performance was good, but the negative behavior remained untouched.

No one remembers what happens in the middle. Consider for a moment that you and two of your coworkers have each been given the opportunity to present a project before the board. Based upon the presentations, only one project will be chosen for funding. Are you going to want to speak first, second, or third? Most people opt for the third or first slot and do anything to avoid the dreaded middle position. Don't allow your message to become the ignored middle child. Get it out there in plain sight, because if your message isn't being heard, you aren't doing anything to resolve the problem.

Positive reinforcement is about being in the moment with something that was done right. Don't waste the opportunity by trying to turn it into a buffer for bad news. If you have to deliver corrections or criticisms, keep it for another time. And make sure that when the employee responds to the criticism and delivers the desirable behavior, you let that employee know, right away and in detail, what he or she did right.

Performance Appraisals

Frequent positive feedback is critical to helping Hundred Percenters achieve their personal best. However, performance appraisals are another story. We conducted a study that showed only 14% of employees feel performance appraisals provide meaningful and relevant feedback.

Despite the fact that these reviews produce minimal results, many organizations still enforce them. If you find yourself in a position where you have no choice but to comply, there are some steps you can take to conduct a more effective performance appraisal. And as a bonus, you may extract some valuable performance information.

Before you go into the meeting, ask employees to give you a list of their proudest moments. This gives you the opportunity to recognize and reward meritorious behavior that you might have missed or forgotten. And that's important, because nothing makes a Hundred Percenter slip into satisficing faster than doing something outstanding and not getting any recognition for it.

The list will also tell you quite a bit about the kind of performer you have. If an employee sets his or her expectations low and expresses pride in making it to work 80% of the time, it tells you something about where this review is likely to be headed.

Putting It Together

Janice is the executive director of a senior living community. She spent the last two decades working her way up the company ladder, and she loves both the organization and her job. Janice commands the respect of her staff and is generally well liked, but she worries that giving out praise will make her look like a pushover.

April, Parker, and Trent are Janice's Hundred Percenters. They're great at what they do, and they love what they do. However, all three share a similar feeling of disappointment that Janice rarely, if ever, provides them with positive feedback. April recently confided in a few of her peers that she's looking for another job. She wants to work for an organization that recognizes her talent and appreciates her efforts.

Workplace grapevines being what they are, Janice quickly caught wind that April, Parker, and Trent were unhappy—and why. As much as it pained her to admit it, Janice realized she was going to have to make some changes in her leadership style. Giving up her command-and-control leadership style, which left little to no room for positive reinforcement, was quite a stretch, but Janice was determined.

She decided to take it a step at a time and see how it went. Trent was working on setting up a calendar of weekly resident outings to places like art galleries, museums, and the theater. Despite working on the project for more than a week, the calendar remained empty. Janice had been considering turning the job over to Parker and had mentioned as much to Trent. She hoped the threat of losing a fun work assignment would act as negative reinforcement and give Trent some incentive to kick it into gear, but it hadn't worked.

She pulled Trent aside and asked him how the job was progressing. It was like someone had let the air out of him. Trent's whole body physically deflated, and his energy just seemed to vanish. But his mind was racing with the following thoughts: Janice had already laid into him twice this week about the stupid calendar. He had about a hundred calls out; it wasn't his fault that nobody was returning them. He was tired of talking about it. Janice had nothing good to say to him, and it was like she was out to get him.

Janice couldn't tell what Trent was thinking, but his silence and body language indicated it wasn't anything good. She jumped right in with the statement she had rehearsed the night before. "I was just looking at your call log. I'm very impressed with the creative thought you've given to this project. We've never had a program coordinator who thought of outings like foreign films and classes at the meditation center. I also see you're trying to get us into the

Degas exhibition at the museum next month. I think our residents will appreciate it. They're always excited about new experiences."

Trent was pleasantly shocked to have Janice speak to him on this level. He actually was enjoying his work on the calendar. He was just frustrated that he couldn't get any results. For the first time he felt like he could trust Janice and ask her for help. It didn't seem like she was going to yell at him. "Yeah, I'm pretty excited about those things too," Trent said. "I actually have a buddy who works at the museum and is trying to get us our own tour guide. I'm just not hearing back from anyone with a definite yes. What do you suggest I do?"

Janice couldn't be happier. It was the first time Trent had asked for her advice. Together they explored some of the ways he could secure dates with his contacts, and he eagerly returned to his desk to get to work.

Later that day, Janice noticed April reviewing the monthly invoices. This was a sore spot around the residence, as invoices always had mistakes and went out late. Janice had made it clear when she delegated this task to April that she wanted it done on time, and miracle of miracles, here she was doing as asked.

Janice jumped right on this opportunity to deliver some positive reinforcement. "April, I can't tell you how thrilled I am that you're reviewing the invoices on schedule. I know you've got other projects going on, and I'm impressed with your ability to schedule yourself so everything gets done. The residents are going to be really happy to get these on time and without error. This goes a long way toward making our organization more professional."

The genuine smile Janice got in response from April told her plenty. Lately it had seemed as if April was never happy. She buried her head in her work and then scurried out at the end of the day. Her performance was good, but her passion had definitely been lacking. Janice could see already that a single hit of positive reinforcement had effected a change in April's attitude.

Since things were going so well, Janice decided to seek out Parker and try a little positive feedback on him. Parker, the youngest member of her team, was inputting into Excel the information she'd given him for next week's schedule. His technical competence was a huge relief for Janice. She'd had to teach some of her employees Excel more times than she cared to remember, and they always got tangled up in some problem with it. "Parker, it's so nice to know I can rely on you to do the schedule," she said. "I really appreciate your ability with Excel."

Parker looked up from his work with a sour look. Janice immediately recognized her error. There was no way Parker was going to take her comment as it was intended. To him, the Excel task was rudimentary work that he was basically stuck with because no one else knew how to do it. If anything, her statement was an insult to his intelligence. She immediately confessed her error by saying, "I don't mean to imply that Excel is the only thing that gives you value around here. I really just wanted you to know that you're doing a good job."

As the words came out, Janice realized she'd blundered again. She'd offered no specific reference to what Parker did that made him so valuable. But then she noticed him smiling; and when he said, "Thanks, Janice. I really do appreciate it," she knew there was an opportunity for another chance. She'd wait for a genuine teachable moment and try again.

Creating Heroes with Storytelling: The Multiplier Technique

Giving Hundred Percenters the positive reinforcement they want and deserve will, on a one-by-one basis, inspire the above-and-beyond performance you want. But what if you could sound a universal call to Hundred Percenter behavior? Make the drive to become a Hundred Percenter viral, infecting your whole workforce with the desire to deliver greater performance. What would it take to get all the members of your staff, from the new summer intern right on up to higher management, to start talking among themselves about the benefits of being a Hundred Percenter?

We call it the multiplier technique, and it's easier to put into effect than you might think. All it takes is a talent you probably, to some extent, already use every day: storytelling. Except instead of talking about the big fish you caught up at the lake or whatever amazing thing your five-year-old accomplished now, you're going to turn the folks who display Hundred Percenter effort into role models, or heroes. It's their stories of achievement you're going to tell. And because of the motivating force of these stories, folks are going to want to talk about them, creating a domino effect that gets your story—and the lesson it teaches—told time and time again.

If it sounds too easy, I'm not surprised. Just as praise has been abused, so has our universal concept of heroes. We look up to our athletes, only to hear drugs helped them achieve the stellar performance we admire. Celebrities and musical talents have risen to superhero proportions, even the ones who have no talent. But how many of them do we see, not just in the supermarket tabloids, but also on our nightly news? And the reports aren't about their charitable efforts, but rather about what naked body part they flashed, the people they're dating, or their involvement in drugs and violence. And it's our continual interest that empowers these folks to maintain their "heroic" status.

It's all well and good to lament the societal decline in what we value and praise, but the time has come to stop complaining and to start doing something to reclaim our real heroes. Storytelling is an ancient tradition that has allowed endless generations to preserve the tales of true heroes. Once upon a time, before reality television, storytelling was all we had. Human beings gathered around the fire, or the radio, or even the television and eagerly tuned in to find out what their favorite hero would do next. Whether it was Odysseus fighting the Trojans or Davy Crockett defending the Alamo, our heroes were the kind of people in whom we could believe. They were folks who were just like us, but who, through discipline and effort, accomplished something outstanding.

Modern-day television and other cultural forces have rendered the power of positive heroes obsolete. Instead of Superman, little boys now want to grow up to be "ganstas," and regardless of age, who doesn't dream of making it big on *Idol*. It's not easy to sit people down and make them listen to a regular old story. Not when their attention is used to being grabbed by multimillion dollar effects that play along to a driving soundtrack and where the boring moments end up on the cutting-room floor. Not to mention reality shows that make viewers believe "stardom could happen to me."

The truth is, reality stars are hardly heroic. The shows are contrived and based on spotlighting dishonorable people doing mean and conniving things. Characters are motivated by greed and lust, and these qualities are enhanced by sound bites and dramatic camera angles. And somewhere in the back of most of our brains, we know it's baloney and that the chances of that reality becoming our own is right up there with winning the lottery. But we still get drawn in to the stories, transported by the drama. And we crave the next episode, because whether it's real or not, we want to see these characters get their just rewards.

All this garbage grips like a vise on a sizable chunk of humanity, which just goes to show you the power of a compelling story. But the real heroes are still out there. They are waiting for us to stop caring whom the most popular bachelor decides to marry— they are waiting for us to come back to our senses and remember that ordinary people doing extraordinary things actually means something important. And chances are, if you take a good look around, you'll find some real-life Hundred Percenter heroes right in your own workplace. These are heroes whose stories will create a buzz and generate positive, viral conversation and behavior.

While I wish it were true, I can't promise that Hundred Percenter stories will wipe out the popularity of reality television and set the world right again. But Hundred Percenter stories will change the focus of the talk around the water cooler from what television's most reviled housewife just did to what Bob in Accounting just did. And that's a kind of celebrity anyone can aspire to—and achieve.

Hundred Percenter Stories

Even though most of us, to some extent, tell stories every day, without some clear direction, the process can be intimidating. How do you start? What do you say next? What if you can't think of a story to tell? What if no one seems to be listening? And for anyone who is used to texting in shorthand, the idea of stringing together an actual start-to-finish story might be frightening. But don't worry, even if your storytelling techniques are rusty or perhaps nonexistent, by the end of this chapter, you'll be a natural.

Hundred Percenter storytelling is not about weaving the most scintillating yarn you can think of. It's got to be interesting enough to hold your listeners' attention, but more important, it has to inspire an emotional reaction that teaches a Hundred Percenter lesson. And the way you can deduce whether or not a story has what it takes to succeed is by looking at how the story ends—before you think about how it begins.

There is a great Hundred Percenter story that has become legendary among employees of the Ritz-Carlton, an organization renowned for inspiring Hundred Percenter effort. The story is good, but the ending is what drives the lesson home. As it's told, a family comes to stay at a Ritz-Carlton Hotel in Bali. The family is traveling with a young child who suffers from food allergies that are so life threatening that the family has to bring its own milk and eggs so the child can eat.

But when the family members arrive at the hotel, they find the food they are carrying is spoiled. A search is made of the island, and no proper food substitutes can be found. The family starts making hurried plans to return home when one of the hotel chefs remembers a market he had seen in Singapore. He is sure this market carries the items the boy needs, and upon placing a call, it's affirmed. He contacts his mother-in-law in Singapore, and she agrees to fly to Bali and deliver the food items. The Ritz-Carlton picks up the cost of the plane ticket, the boy gets his food, and the chef gets an unplanned visit from his mother-in-law.

The reason this story is so effective is because any employee who hears it also hears the lesson that "at the Ritz-Carlton, we go above and beyond." Granted, not everyone has family in the same place as that chef, but the actions he took are repeatable behaviors, and they fit the Hundred Percent effort the Ritz demands of its employees, folks who are trained under the motto "We are Ladies and Gentlemen serving Ladies and Gentlemen." This is the story of one gentleman doing for others.

The year 1997 marked the passing of two remarkable women, Diana, Princess of Wales, and Mother Teresa of Calcutta. They died within days of each other, and the media made much of their similarities. But the fact is, aside from the charitable activities they took part in, these women could not have been more different.

Princess Diana may have been known as the People's Princess, but the very real fact remains that she was a princess, a title not many of us get to hold in our lifetimes. Typically, for a "commoner," the journey toward becoming a princess starts at birth. You're born into an elite crowd, you know the right people, you wear the right things, and you go to the right places. You know not everyone in your group is going to get the gold ring, but you also know if you play your cards right, you've got a fighting chance of marrying a prince.

On the other hand, there's Mother Teresa. Unlike Diana, she was born into average circumstances. She wasn't pushed to greatness as part of her birthright. Rather, she made an independent choice to do something extraordinary with her life. This is not to dismiss or undercut the great things Diana accomplished during her lifetime. But when you look at which of these two women is the more viable hero for the "everyman"—which of their behaviors would be easier to duplicate—hands down, Mother Teresa wins.

Ironically, the media coverage of Princess Diana, her life, and her death was a hundred times greater than the media coverage given to Mother Teresa. But the media had a different intention in creating their multiplier effect. Even though both women accomplished amazing things, let's face it, it's a whole lot more glamorous to be a princess than a poor nun. Diana's story guaranteed better ratings. But what if the media's primary focus had been on Mother Teresa? Instead of dreaming of tiaras and ball gowns, the "common folk" might instead have been inspired to think about how they could do their own best work and give more of themselves to the world to make it a better place.

When you set out to create a Hundred Percenter story, look for a Mother Teresa story, one that anyone can replicate, and not an out-of-reach Princess Di story. The time the garbage in the lunchroom caught fire, and Carl from marketing rushed in with a fire extinguisher and saved the day, is a great story. The problem is that it's a story that is a once-in-a-lifetime event (we hope!). However, the time Carl worked through the weekend to fully implement a new brand for the company teaches a Hundred Percenter lesson other people can apply to their own day-to-day work. You'll know the stories that have the greatest teaching potential when their endings are in synch with the behaviors you need most from your people.

If you're wondering where on earth you are supposed to find your Hundred Percenter stories, the answer is, right in front of you. Take some time to observe what is going on in your workplace. Go out to your front lines and talk to your people. Poke around for details that can be "sexed up" and made into engaging stories. Solicit your team, your managers, your customers by asking, "Tell me about a time when you, or another employee, or someone in this organization really knocked it out of the park." Then determine if anything you hear reinforces the specific, controllable, Hundred Percenter behavior you want to see replicated.

Don't just look to your proven Hundred Percenters to find fodder for your stories. It's important to cast the storytelling spotlight evenly on both known high performers and surprise performers: satisficers who pulled off a Hundred Percenter move. This serves the dual purpose of keeping your current Hundred Percenters motivated and working at top form and inspiring your satisficers to reach for more. The goal is to turn as many folks as you can into heroes, as long as they deserve it.

The Rules of Great Storytelling

Not everyone is a born storyteller. So we've created some Storytelling Rules that will help you create Hundred Percenter stories that have what it takes to go viral.

Storytelling Rule #1: Use Experiential Language

A great story draws listeners in by showing, not telling, the course of events. Telling is just the dry communication of facts and figures, and even an extraordinary tale will be boring if that's all you give. People want more than hard data. They want to have an emotional connection to a story. If it's relative to experiences they already know, something they can see, hear, feel, or otherwise relate to, you'll have them hooked. And just like reading a great novel, while your listeners wait to find out what happens next, they'll be putting themselves in the hero's shoes, thinking about how it feels to be in that situation and how they too could become a hero who accomplishes the same Hundred Percenter results.

Experiential language is a key function of storytelling, and unlike the author of a novel, you have an advantage: the intimate knowledge of your audience and the exact emotional response you want to elicit from them.

There are two reliable methods of drawing your listeners into the story:

1. Five senses: sight, touch, smell, taste, and sound
2. Five core emotions: mad, sad, glad, afraid, and ashamed

First, let's take a look at a story that *tells* instead of *shows*. Here, the CEO of the advertising agency tells how an employee, Paul, recognized a chance to go above and beyond.

"Paul had been with the company for a year when our head of marketing quit, right in the middle of carrying out a big campaign for an important client. Everyone thought the project was a lost cause, but Paul, who had been helping with the campaign, said he could finish the work. The rest is history."

Now let's look the same story when the CEO *shows* what happened rather than *tells* it.

"Paul's story is what I would call a sleeper success story; it was totally unexpected. In the first year he worked here, you didn't hear much from Paul. He showed up, did his work just fine, and went home. Then, our head of marketing ups and quits with no notice—

right in the middle of a huge campaign for a new client. That's when we got to see the real Paul in action.

"As you can imagine, it was bedlam in the office with everyone scrambling around to pick up the pieces. Except for Paul, who 100% kept his cool. He marches into my office and stands there just spouting confidence. It was like he had grown a foot in the last 10 minutes. 'I can carry this campaign,' he said, and there wasn't a speck of hesitation in his voice. I knew what he would be up against. The client was unsure about using us and was expecting us to jump through a lot of hoops to win his favor.

"Paul really wanted the chance, and he made me believe he could do it. So I let him run with it, and boy did he run. You folks all know who that client was—it's the same client who pays most of your salaries today. Thanks to Paul, the client's remained our most loyal and successful account."

Storytelling Rule #2: Six Steps

Great stories that go viral don't just happen; they are made. By building on the following six steps, your story will have all the right elements.

> *Step #1: Set the scene.* Where did the action in your story take place? If it's the very same spot from which you are telling the story, that's got impact, as does the selling-room floor, the boardroom, or any number of places. Put your listeners fully in the moment by making them visualize exactly what it looked like the day the story took place.
>
> *Step #2: Expand on your protagonist.* Even though everyone may know who "Dan from the third floor" is, it's critical to give Dan greater dimension. If folks are going to be drawn to repeat Dan's behavior, they need to key in to how they are "just like him." Include at least one fact that

makes your hero relevant to everyone. For example, "It was Dan's first day," or "Dan had been with the company for 20 years when . . ."

Step #3: What is the goal, and why is it worthwhile? The protagonist of your story certainly didn't go above and beyond for no good reason. There was a goal that sent him or her on this heroic quest, and when listeners know that goal, it removes any suspicion that the purpose was a narcissistic reward. Don't leave it to your listeners to deduce for themselves why the Hundred Percenter effort took place. This isn't a story that's open to interpretation.

Step #4: Struggle. Unless your protagonist had some obstacles to overcome, the quest won't have much meaning. Struggles don't have to be bigger than life to have impact. A new parent who is exhausted from having a new baby, and who nevertheless puts in an all-nighter to get an important project done, faces an admirable struggle. What's more, it's a struggle that is relevant to a lot of folks.

Step #5: Resolution. Hundred Percenter stories always have a happy ending. The resolution of your story should clearly show listeners that working for goals bigger than yourself has widespread benefit.

Step #6: What if? The "what if" is a tag intended to reinforce how extraordinary the action taken by the protagonist was. Mention what would have happened if the hero had not overcome the obstacles and achieved the goal. It doesn't have to be life or death consequences to be impactful.

Let's take a look at how the manager of a rental equipment store applied the six steps to tell a Hundred Percenter story that went viral in his organization: "Do you guys remember that huge ice storm we had three years ago? That's the day we gained our biggest customer.

The whole city was shut down. We had maybe a quarter of the staff who made it in that day. This place was like a ghost town. That morning we get a call from the local hospital. The emergency generators weren't working right. The hospital wants to know what we can send over and how quickly we can get it there.

"Jason is the one who got the call. And boy was he fast on his feet, which, when you consider he'd been living here in town and with the company for only six months, is really something. He knew those people were in peril if he didn't act fast. I mean, the whole hospital was about to be plunged into total darkness, paralyzing its critical-support systems.

"Within minutes, Jason organized the few people on staff into teams. We had only seven generators available, but he sent the rest of our people out to the other rental places in town to get the generators they had. It was tough going, the roads were impossible, and the police had everything shut down. But under Jason's leadership, power was restored to the hospital, and no patients suffered any complications. I don't even want to think about the consequences and what those people might have suffered if Jason had not done what he did."

Storytelling Rule #3: The Follow-Up

Some Hundred Percenter stories will take off like wildfire, while others might need a little push to get going. Either way, you want to do your part to keep the story alive. I suggest two methods of doing this. The first is sparking a conversation with your people right after you tell the story. A question as simple as "What can each of us do to create a similar story?" will get the mental juices flowing. You might even get some information that leads to new stories, such as an employee who says, "Hey, remember that time the company mechanic was out sick and I fixed the delivery truck myself? That's sort of the same kind of story."

The other method is to incorporate these stories into daily or weekly meetings. The Ritz-Carlton conducts its famous daily line-ups, where every employee participates in a 15-minute meeting to discuss the obvious (like which king or prime minister is checking in that day), but also to review their Gold Standards and the stories that exemplify them.

Other clients conduct daily huddles or weekly reviews, where 10 minutes is devoted to highlighting one of these Hundred Percenter stories. The key is to tell the stories regularly (never assume people know them) so that you set a high bar for performance and teach people exactly what they need to do to clear that bar.

Conclusion

I began the chapter by identifying two of the bad lessons we're teaching our employees:

Lesson #1: Being a Hundred Percenter stinks.
Lesson #2: The boss can't tell the difference between
　　Hundred Percenters and Fifty Percenters.

Employees learn from other employees, and given how we typically treat our Hundred Percenters, the lessons aren't great. But when we harness the power of positive reinforcement and use the multiplicative impact of viral stories to spread that positivity, we start to teach very different lessons:

Lesson #1: Being a Hundred Percenter gets noticed.
Lesson #2: Being a Hundred Percenter gets rewarded.
Lesson #3: There are very specific and teachable steps to
　　becoming a Hundred Percenter.

4

Stop Demotivating and Start Motivating

One of the reasons 100% Leaders are so successful at getting employees to meet and surpass hard challenges is because they establish connections that inspire their people to aspire to greatness. However, 100% Leaders are never Appeasers (the kind of leaders who send the message, "You only have to do work you like; everything you are doing is terrific; I want to do whatever it takes to make you happy"). Appeasing isn't leading; it's placating. It will never make you feel genuinely good about your leadership skills, and it won't create even a ripple in the status quo. You might as well throw your HARD goals in the trash and cater a party to celebrate your "great" team that will never get any better.

The message that 100% Leaders send is "Yes, I expect Hundred Percenter performance from you, but I also care about your success and fulfillment." If you recall, the first critical lesson of being a 100% Leader is, if the status quo felt bad, people would have changed already. If your people have been coasting by with moderate effort, decent results, and even minimal praise, where's the incentive to do anything differently? If you are going to change the status quo and ask for Hundred Percenter performance, you need to back it up with some solid evidence that being a Hundred Percenter is worth the extra effort. And that's exactly what Shoves and Tugs deliver.

Hundred Percenters aren't organizational Old Faithfuls. They don't spout above-and-beyond performance—on demand—simply because that's the kind of people they are. You can't deliver a HARD goal and expect even your best people to leap on it with excitement, unless they have a reason to jump. As one of our favorite clients (a reformed Intimidator) wisely remarked, "A frog can't jump if you are standing on its legs."

Hundred Percenters come with a predisposition to jump toward greatness. Thanks to myriad factors that happened long before they walked through your doors (such as a good upbringing with nurturing parents and caring teachers), these folks pack an arsenal of desirable qualities—things like a strong competitive drive, high motivation, and an intuitive understanding of your definition of success, just the kind of jumping you want. But if you've got their legs pinned to the ground, either because they feel totally intimidated or because you're killing them with kindness that says, "No need to jump; you're doing just fine there on the ground," they aren't going anywhere. And they especially aren't jumping toward greater success.

Granted, Hundred Percenters are a good deal more sophisticated than frogs, but you still need to give them an environment that's prime for jumping. And that means both enticing your people to jump high and far and clearing out the demotivators that keep them firmly lodged in the status quo—or worse.

"I've got this one covered," says Doug, who manages an IT department for a well-known university. "No one offers the kind of incentives we do. I'm talking flexible work schedules, tuition waivers, birthday breakfasts—tons of organizational swag—and you've gotta see the spread at our Christmas parties. My people are jumping with joy!"

It all sounds good until you talk to Mary, one of Doug's top performers. She loves the work, but admits it's getting harder and harder to feel excited about the job. "The new flexible work schedule is a real downer," says Mary. "Used to be I had everything timed around my kids' schedules, but with my new 'flexible' hours, it's a total mess." Mary also resents all the social gatherings. "Last week I faked an emergency at home so I could cut out early and avoid another birthday party. Enough is enough," she says. "Speaking of which, please, no more shirts or baseball hats spotlighting the university mascot. I don't have any more room for all this junk."

Does Money Work?

You can give Hundred Percenters a round-trip ticket to the moon, but if it's not what they want, you're not inspiring them to jump. In fact, you might even be pushing them toward rolling over and basking in the sweetness of the status quo. The good news is, the motivators most Hundred Percenters want aren't tied to money. And the same goes for the employees who, with a little added incentive, will make the leap to Hundred Percenter performance. That's not to say money doesn't have a motivational impact, especially if your people are paid below market. But if you look at the reasons why people check out of their jobs, study after study shows money has little to do with professional happiness.

For the sake of argument, let's say Mary makes $30,000 a year. While browsing a popular Internet job board, she sees a similar position at a college across town that would include a 15% pay increase. This doesn't sound bad until you do the math. A 15% increase would give Mary $4,500 more a year, roughly $375 extra a month—before taxes. After taxes, she might have enough to pay for an extra tank of gas every week, exactly what she'll need to cover the extra distance to the new job and back.

This might be enough to push Mary out the door if she really hates her current job or thinks the boss, Doug, is a huge jerk. If every day is an emotional roller-coaster of things that make her jump out of her skin with annoyance and misery, she'd probably be happy to take the new job for a pay decrease. However, if Doug were to give Mary some perks that make her happy, and take away some of the factors that make her miserable, a tank of gas isn't going to be enough to lure Mary away from her current job.

"But wait just a minute," you might be saying. "All the employees I've ever given an exit interview to have told me they quit because of money. Are you telling me they all lied?" The answer is, for the most part, yes. It's no different from the old breakup excuse, "It's me, not you." Most people don't want to sit face-to-face with someone, whether an ex-lover or an ex-boss, and say, "Look, you're an idiot. Just talking to you makes me want to scream, and I probably will do just that if I don't get out of here in the next five minutes." And even if an employee does have the gall to tell you what he or she thinks of you, on a practical level you might be handy as a reference down the line. So there's major negative benefit in telling the truth. Using money as an excuse is the best way to slip out on relatively good terms.

Bottom line, money is great, but few organizations can continually (and legally) offer the kind of money that really makes a difference. What they can offer is all the other stuff that gets and keeps Hundred Percenters, and Hundred Percenter hopefuls, feeling excited and motivated and striving to attain HARD goals.

If there's one hallmark of 100% Leaders, it's pragmatism. They take nothing for granted, and they don't stand on ceremony. They find out exactly what their best people want, and if it's practical and possible, they make it happen. They also find out what these folks don't want, and if they can't make it go away, they try to neutralize the problem. And as you are about to find out, that doesn't mean trying to mask the negative stuff with perks.

No Such Thing as Average

So what exactly does the average Hundred Percenter want? That's a great question that comes with a loaded answer. I know sports parables aren't everyone's favorite, but I'm going to use one anyway to make a point. I was raised in Buffalo, New York, and even though I now live down south, I remain a die-hard Buffalo Bills fan. I once read that the average NFL player weighs 245 pounds and stands at 6 feet 1½ inches tall. But when I looked into it, I couldn't find a single player on the Buffalo Bills who weighs 245 pounds or who stands at 6 feet 1½ inches tall. Hence, there is no player who matches both averages (i.e., weighs 245 pounds and is 6 feet 1½ inches tall).

I was investigating the reliability of averages for another project, and my curiosity naturally grew. I assigned one of my researchers to scour the rosters of every NFL team, looking for the average player (who, as noted above, would weigh 245 pounds and measure 6 feet 1½ inches tall). It was pretty tedious work, and so I let him stop after 10 teams. As you might guess, he was unable to find even one player who matched the NFL average.

The point of all this is that averages are misleading. Nobody is "average," and if you go looking for the "average" person, you will probably never find him or her. (Have you ever seen a family with 2.5 kids?) This same "fallacy of the average person" holds true when we're talking about Hundred Percenters. What they want—and what they don't want—is as unique and individual as is what you want—and don't want.

Mary isn't interested in all the perks Doug finds so enticing. She doesn't want flexible shifts. However, she does want greater opportunity for career advancement and work that provides greater challenge. She'd also like fewer social gatherings and far less interaction with low performers. Then there's Bill, another top performer, who works with Mary and who loves the new flexible work schedule. Bill does wish that the job offered better benefits and that Doug was less of a micromanager. And while he loves all the social gatherings, he often finds himself feeling isolated in his work, and that isn't the kind of environment that pushes him to give more.

Mary and Bill are just two examples of how the concept of "different strokes for different folks" comes into play in the workplace. In the book *The War for Talent*, consultants from McKinsey & Company asked thousands of managers and executives, "What are the critical factors in your decision to join and stay at an organization?" The answers were all over the place.

Some folks said interesting and challenging work; others said it's work they feel passionate about. Some said it's career advancement opportunities; others said it's the company's long-term commitment to them. Other popular answers included a well-managed company, good relationships with the boss, appreciation of the culture and values, the appealing physical location, a reasonable work pace, higher pay for higher performers, and a high annual cash compensation. McKinsey's total list comprised around 40 issues.

Exit interview studies showed similar results. In organization-wide studies people usually say they quit for reasons that include lack of recognition or rewards, insufficient advancement opportunities, inadequate or no feedback from management, feelings of not being valued as an employee, few or no opportunities for training and education, uncompetitive compensation, and lack of responsibility.

If you can distill these responses into one universal factor that motivates employees to deliver stellar performance, you deserve a medal. We've tried, and it just doesn't work. People are unique, and they are driven by different things. But most organizations still haven't gotten the message. Every day we see companies implement organization-wide strategies that utilize a limited number of motivational techniques to inspire improved performance (desperately hoping to find that "average" employee).

It's not that those "average" techniques don't work. They'll certainly work for some of your employees. But if a patient arrived in the emergency room suffering from 40 stab wounds, are we going to treat only 1 of those wounds and hope that the other 39 will take care of themselves?

Some People Don't Know

There's one more complicating factor we have to address. There are a decent number of cases where people just don't know what makes them motivated or demotivated. Take Craig, for example. He is a highly gifted programmer and potential Hundred Percenter, and as a performance "reward," he got promoted to manager. The organization even threw him a party to celebrate the step up. Craig never aspired to be a manager, but with all the attention he got over it, he figured the promotion couldn't be anything but great.

The problem is that Craig has no leadership skills, a factor his boss failed to take into account when rewarding Craig for his great performance. Craig's true talent, the place where he could be a

Hundred Percenter, is in programming. Consequently, Craig went from achieving great success to experiencing failure after failure. He started to believe that it was his fault and that he just wasn't good enough. It didn't take long for Craig to fall into a pit of hopelessness that kept him from delivering any effort at all. He started thinking about quitting the organization.

Aren't There Any Universal Motivators?

I think I've made the point that you can't run around giving everybody gift cards or flexible work schedules and expect that your motivating work is complete. But there is a factor we all seem to want: a boss who listens to our unique concerns—good and bad. We want to know somebody is paying attention to the factors that get us revved up, and that somebody has the guts to listen to us when we're facing a situation that is emotionally killing us.

It's entirely likely that at any given time, many members of your team are going to be motivated or demotivated by a similar set of issues. After all, they share the same boss, and they could be working on the same project or with the same customers. The point isn't that you will never see common motivational themes; it's that even if you do see common themes, those themes could change from week to week, from month to month, from project to project, from department to department.

There's only one approach that reliably and dynamically identifies what your people want and what they don't want: the two factors that will inspire them to give—and keep on giving—Hundred Percenter effort. You must engage them in a one-to-one conversation and ask them outright. We call this conversation Shoves and Tugs.

Shoves and Tugs

Everybody has Shoves and Tugs. Shoves are those issues that demotivate you, drain your energy, stop you from giving Hundred Percenter effort, and make you want to quit—they "shove" you out the door. Tugs are those issues that motivate and fulfill you, make you want to give Hundred Percenter effort, and keep you coming back every day—they "tug" at you to stay.

This seems simple enough. But here's the twist: Shoves and Tugs are *not* flip sides of the same coin. Just because somebody has lots of Tugs coming up this week does *not* mean they don't have any Shoves. And before you can spend all day trying to figure out how to give people lots of Tugs, you've got to at least acknowledge (and ideally mitigate) their Shoves.

Let me begin with an analogy that's a little "out there," but that might help clarify this issue. Much like Shoves and Tugs are not opposites of each other, so too are pain and pleasure not opposites of each other. The opposite of pleasure isn't pain; it's just the absence of pleasure. Similarly, the opposite of pain isn't pleasure; it's just the absence of pain. If somebody is hitting my foot with a hammer, that's pain. And when the hammering stops, that's not pleasure; that's just no more pain. If I'm getting the world's greatest back rub, that's pleasure. When it stops, that's not pain; that's just no more pleasure.

Here's the lesson: If I'm getting a great back rub, it does *not* preclude somebody from starting to hit my foot with a hammer. And if that happens, the pain in my foot will totally detract from the pleasure I'm getting from the back rub. Here's a corollary lesson: If you walk past me one day and see that my foot is being hit with a hammer, you *cannot* fix the pain in my foot by giving me a back rub. The only way to stop the pain in my foot is to stop the hammer from hitting it.

I told you this was a weird analogy, but here's why it's relevant. Every day, in organizations around the world, employees' feet are being hit with hammers, and their boss's solution isn't to stop the hammer (i.e., eliminate the Shove), but rather to offer a back rub (i.e., offer a Tug).

Consider, for example, a software development team in Silicon Valley led by a manager named Chris. The department was on heavy deadline to finish a new product, and more than a few of the organization's Hundred Percenters were frustrated with the situation. Recently Chris's anxiety had caused him to start micromanaging (and instituting numerous meetings widely acknowledged as useless). He was also concerned because one of the low performers on the team had complained about the emotional intensity in the department, and so he decided everyone would have to take a one-hour lunch together to decompress. The net effect was that the Hundred Percenters were having to make up the work at home.

As often happens, Chris's actions caused even more grumbling. As the grumbling hit a fever pitch, rather than ask the members of his team about the source of their frustration, Chris decided to take the whole team to Catalina Island for the weekend to relax. He figured it was a great way to offer a nice reward and get everyone's brains back into the game. When he made the announcement, more than a few of the programmers' heads nearly exploded. The last thing they wanted was more time with one other just hanging out and not working. They wanted to finish the project, to hit the deadline, and then to go home and see their families. They wanted to stop wasting time at work and just get the job done.

Chris made the mistake of trying to fix a Shove with a Tug, and it couldn't have backfired more. Yes, Catalina Island is beautiful, and perhaps in another circumstance it would have been a nice reward. But his team was getting Shoved by too much time away from the actual work of programming, and here comes the boss with a Tug that involves more time away from programming. Not only was the Tug a poor choice, but Chris's credibility is shot; he seems obtuse and insensitive for not understanding what was really demoralizing his team.

It was the same situation for a hospital experiencing a major nursing shortage. Management implemented mandatory overtime, which made everyone tired and stressed. In an effort to make things better, management threw a big picnic for the nurses, something that in the past, before the shortage, had made the nurses really happy.

Only in the face of the obvious Shoves, the Tug didn't work. Attendance at the picnic was sparse, and those who did attend could be heard saying things like, "Why couldn't they have taken the money they wasted on this picnic and hired a new nurse?" and "Do they really think they can buy us off with a picnic as though we were five-year-olds? Do they really think we can't tell the difference?"

When good employees are working with low performers, or they're fighting through roadblocks, or they've got a terrible working environment, whatever the Shoves may be, it's like getting hit on the foot with a hammer. Great things (Tugs) like autonomy, the ability to have control over an entire process, and the ability to work on innovative projects and teams aren't going to mean a thing until you take away the pain.

What Do You Actually Ask?

A Shoves and Tugs conversation doesn't have to be formal; in fact, it's actually better if it's not. The last thing you want is to make it seem like a performance appraisal. The first rule is, get out from behind your desk. I suggest holding your Shoves and Tugs conversations over coffee or lunch, anywhere two people can have a reasonably private conversation for at least 20 minutes. And just to be clear, we're also talking about a conversation that takes place at least once every quarter (although once a month is even better).

In the majority of cases, two simple questions are all you need to ask:

1. Tell me about a time in the past month or two when you felt demotivated (or frustrated, or emotionally burned out, or whatever words sound like something you would say).
2. Tell me about a time in the past month or two when you felt motivated (or excited, or jazzed up, or however you might naturally express this).

Bear in mind that you're not asking these questions simply for the sake of asking questions; you actually want to know the answers. And what you'll typically find is that the issues raised by these questions are as different as people's hair color or their choice of ties. Each person is a little bit different, so find out exactly what will drive each individual to jump to Hundred Percenter performance and what is keeping that person firmly lodged in the status quo.

Maybe you're wondering why we can't ask these questions in the abstract (e.g., what are some things that might demotivate you?). If you were to ask me what might demotivate me, I could give you a list of 101 things. And I might not even mention the ones that are demotivating me in the here and now (because as bad as the demotivators are that I'm currently experiencing, I could probably imagine worse). When you ask people to imagine things, you will get exactly what you asked for—an imaginary list. What you need to know are the factors that are happening right here and now. It's rare for someone to stop giving Hundred Percenter effort because of a demotivator that hasn't yet happened. But lots of people will stop giving Hundred Percenter effort because of demotivators they're experiencing this week.

It's natural to wonder if asking these questions will make employees think twice about all the demotivators they face. Could you be putting negative ideas in their heads? Look, just because you have an EKG at a checkup doesn't mean you're more likely to have a heart attack. If you get screened for breast or prostate cancer, it doesn't mean you're more likely to get those cancers.

If you're at risk of a heart attack, getting a good cardiac workup will uncover that hidden risk. It may feel scary to learn that your risk is so high (and that's why so many people don't get the necessary tests), but the tests don't cause the illness. So the real question is, do you want to bury your head in the sand or do you want a team of Hundred Percenters?

Assess the Conversation

There are clues in both the Shoves and Tugs answers employees give that allow you to assess how the conversation is progressing and whether you need to push for more information.

There are four levels to look for:

1. *Superficial level.* This is when the employee answers, "Everything is fine. I can't think of anything." This person is actively avoiding the issue. We all can point to a time in the past 90 days when something either pleased us or ticked us off.
2. *Suspicious level.* If you hear something like, "I'm sure there are things, but why do you want to know?" it shows the employee has an awareness of issues he or she

is not denying, but fears that revealing those issues might result in trouble or even getting fired.

3. *Involved level.* If you learn about a specific problem, probably not pertaining to you, but the employee offers no recommended solution, there's clear evidence of a Shove. But there is still a level of distrust. This employee wants evidence of how far you are willing to go to fix the situation before he or she will feel safe to spill the beans.

4. *Committed level.* If the employee gives you a full-blown description of a Shove, even if it pertains to you, and tells you what specifically should be done to fix it, you've hit the Shoves and Tugs jackpot.

If you find yourself stuck at the superficial level, it's probably an indication that you don't have a great history with this person. You might get the employee to loosen up a bit if you change the focus to a third-person approach. It's always safer to talk about your own stuff when you pretend it belongs to someone else. To make the shift into third person, ask a question such as:

What are the two to three things you think other employees like best about this organization?

What are the two to three things you think other employees like least about this organization?

Can you imagine reasons why employees would leave this company?

When your Shoves and Tugs conversation isn't going as well as you'd like, repetition is the key to get it on track. If you talk to 10 employees and only one person tells you a Shove—perhaps the person reports a distaste for being micromanaged, especially on repetitive tasks—you've got something to work with. Let everyone witness your efforts to rein in your tendencies to micromanage. If your organization is like most, the news of "Wow, she didn't fire me! She actually did what I asked!" will hit the grapevine in about two milliseconds. The following month, when you have your next set of Shoves and Tugs talks, you'll get a few more employees who will feel safe to test the waters. Eventually you'll gain most people's trust.

There's one tactic that will absolutely destroy all your efforts and make every one of your employees defensive and closed mouth. It takes courage to tell the boss, "Well, sometimes you micromanage me, and it really turns me off." The fact may be that the person describing this Shove needs to be micromanaged from time to time. However, if you come back with a comment like, "Well, if you didn't screw up so much, I wouldn't have to micromanage you," the only thing you'll do is shut down any chance of productive communication. It takes practice to hold your tongue when you're being bopped over the head with an accusation that couldn't be more off track. But a Shoves and Tugs conversation isn't about how you feel or why you (or the organization) act the way you do. For that moment, it's all about the other person. So get used to calmly nodding your head and saying, "I hear you."

There will be Shoves that are outside your control and you simply can't fix. But be careful not to jump to this conclusion just because you don't see an immediate or obvious way out. Listen to what your employees tell you. The person talking about the Shove is the one living that Shove, and so chances are good that he or she has given it a lot of thought, including what can be done to fix it. If there truly is nothing that can be done to eliminate or neutralize the Shove, the only recourse is honesty. Don't lie and say, "Right, well, it might take me six or eight months to be able to swing that, but I'll work on it," hoping it all gets swept under the rug and forgotten. Unaddressed Shoves don't get forgotten; they only get worse.

It's Too Easy

If the idea of sitting down with employees and asking a few questions to diagnose individual motivational drivers sounds too easy, you're not alone in thinking that. If that's all it takes to keep Hundred Percenters on track and to get potential Hundred Percenters to take the leap, wouldn't everyone already be doing it? It seems like commonsense logic, but our studies show that fewer than 25% of leaders actually engage in the kind of one-on-one conversation Shoves and Tugs require.

One reason why people often don't choose the easy way is that complicated solutions come with a built-in excuse for failure. That's an attractive safety net for leaders who fear that public failure (with no fallback on which to lay the blame) could reduce their power or even cost them their jobs. It's not much different from weight loss. Whether we admit it or not, most of us intuitively know that a regimen that consists of a healthy diet and moderate exercise is the best way to lose weight. And what could be simpler. Yet if you look at all the popular weight-loss systems and fancy exercise equipment for sale, it's easy to see that most people aren't interested in taking the easy—and effective—route.

It may seem unappealing to live on only cabbage soup for two weeks just to drop a few pounds. Certainly, it would be a lot easier to stop eating junk food, incorporate a few more salads into your life, and take a walk a few times a week. But how do you justify it if you fail? If you drop off the cabbage soup diet, you look like a hero for even trying something that impossible. If you slip up and eat fast food for lunch one day and skip taking your daily walk, you're just lazy. Complicated solutions dangle an element of difficulty that makes them the perfect target for blame if you don't succeed.

Another appealing aspect of complicated solutions is that they allow us to avoid dealing with the truth. It's easy to sit down with an employee and say, "So, Joe, what do you love and what do you hate about the job?" However, it's not always easy to hear what Joe has to say. It's the same reason why women over 40 don't get enough mammograms, and men over 50 don't get enough PSA tests. What if you get bad news? If you don't know about the problem, it's like it doesn't exist. Only it does, and if you don't do anything about it, it's not going to go away; it's going to get worse.

Don't think you can fudge the conversation and ask only about the Tugs, the things that make people happy and inspire Hundred Percenter performance. You need to find out about both Shoves and Tugs. Because if you don't find out what frustrates folks enough to potentially shove them out the door, it won't matter what you lay at their feet to try and tug them to stay; it won't mean a thing, and it may even backfire on you. Before you can inspire folks to give more, you've got to wipe away, or at least neutralize, the things that make them give less.

And for anyone who still might be thinking it's possible to avoid the "easy way out," don't get any ideas about just creating a working environment free from Shoves and forgetting about the Tugs. Your Hundred Percenters aren't going to perform their best if they are being shoved, but neither are they if there is nothing tugging at them to which they can give their all.

Before we move on, I want to address one excuse I hear more than any other for avoiding the Shoves and Tugs conversation: "I don't have the time to sit around with all 10 (or 30, or 50—whatever the number) of my employees and talk about this fuzzy stuff." The fact is, a productive Shoves and Tugs conversation takes no more than 15 to 30 minutes, less time than you probably spend drinking coffee every day. You don't have to talk to every employee in a single day. Talk to one a day, and in a month or so you'll have worked through all 30. And by the time you reach number 30, you'll already have made some progress turning the first 20 into Hundred Percenters.

Shoves and Tugs for Seven Different Personalities

Now that we've got the Shoves and Tugs model down pat, let's advance the science a bit more. As you get to really know your employees, you'll notice that certain types of personalities are going to express similar kinds of Shoves and Tugs. People who are always looking for that next adrenaline rush might tell you about Shoves where they were extremely bored or where they were stymied in their attempt to implement some new cutting-edge improvement. People who love solving problems might be getting Tugs from working on salvaging projects that others have abandoned.

Just because people have similar personality types and motivational drivers does not mean that their Shoves and Tugs will be exactly the same. After all, they could be working in different situations with different people on different projects, etc. But you will likely start to hear some similar types of Shoves and Tugs, and if you know what personality types tend to like or dislike certain situations, you can be better prepared in your Shoves and Tugs conversations.

There are hundreds of theories on personality types, but when it comes to workplace behavior, we've found there are seven driving needs that influence who people are and what they like and dislike:

1. Achievement
2. Power
3. Affiliation

4. Security
5. Reward
6. Adventure
7. Actualization

Let's take a look at how all seven come into play through a study of seven employees, all of whom hold senior marketing positions at StayHealthyInc., an international (fictional, but based on our real-life research) fitness franchise. All seven subjects are around 40 years old, they all have kids, they all drink coffee, they're all married, they've all tried Atkins and South Beach diets, they all went to college and graduate school, and they are all potential Hundred Percenters. In short, these folks are pretty demographically similar. But that doesn't mean they're motivated or demotivated by the same things. Let's take a look.

Achievement

Grace's excitement about the job increases as her responsibilities grow. She's a risk taker who doesn't care much about recognition. She gets her high from the satisfaction of giving superior performance. Cream puff work that is repetitive or menial frustrates her and greatly decreases the effort she gives to the job. Given the choice of working in a group or on her own, she will always choose going solo unless she is partnered with someone who is just like her.

People like Grace, with a high need for achievement, seek to excel. Predominantly achievement-motivated individuals avoid low-risk situations because the easily attained success is not a genuine achievement. These individuals prefer work that has a moderate probability of success. Achievement-motivated individuals want regular feedback in order to monitor the progress of their achievements. They prefer to work either alone or with others like themselves (see Table 4-1).

Table 4-1. High need for achievement

Common Tugs	Common Shoves
Difficult tasks	Tasks that are too easy or
Lots of feedback	that are repetitive
Praise	Tasks with no measurable
Evaluations	outcome
Working alone	Working with low
Working with other	performers
achievers	
Getting to choose tasks,	
or work, or projects	
Becoming a "specialist" at	
a task or job	

Power

Whether it pertains to her own work area and product or her coworkers, Sue needs power, usually in the form of control. To some people, she can come off as bossy and territorial, but she's very competent. When she's in control, she's highly motivated. If she lost that control, she'd lose her desire to work for StayHealthyInc.

Folks like Sue need personal power. They want to be in charge, and they crave the authority to make decisions that will impact others. The need for power also means wanting to be well regarded and to be followed. Power-motivated individuals typically do not respond well to being told what to do or how to do it—unless it comes from a person they wish to emulate (see Table 4-2).

Table 4-2. High need for power

Common Tugs	Common Shoves
Responsibility	Micromanagement
Recognition	Fuzzy organizational
Making clear the path to	structure
advancement	Shared decision making
Job titles	
Leading projects	

Affiliation

Everyone knows Rory; he's a team player through and through. Nothing motivates him to improve organizational systems, solve problems, and find new opportunities more than working in a group environment. He's got a gift for infusing both coworkers and clients with positive energy and for pulling people together to achieve a common goal. If you give him a project where he might step on some of his coworkers' feet, don't be surprised if he passes.

Employees like Rory have a high need for affiliation. They want harmonious relationships, and they want to feel accepted by other people. These individuals prefer work that provides significant personal interaction. They enjoy being part of groups and make excellent team members, though sometimes are distractible into social interaction. They can perform particularly well in customer service and client interaction situations (see Table 4-3).

Table 4-3. High need for affiliation

Common Tugs	Common Shoves
Teamwork	Solo work
Jobs with much social	Isolation
contact	Office physically distant
Face-to-face time	from others
Committees	
Extracurricular activities	

Security

Paul is driven by having a clear job role and taking on only sure bets. He doesn't want rapid change or high-risk opportunities. If it hasn't been done before or if he can't see it in writing, he's not interested. If you invite him in on a project by saying, "I'm not sure how you fit into this team yet, but come on board and we'll figure it out as we go," you're going to send Paul scurrying for safety.

Paul and others like him have a high need for security and look for continuity in their work life. They may prefer to stay with the same company, or in the same position or department, for the long haul. They are driven by guarantees. High-security people get anxious over change. They value consistency in their job, work, and pay (see Table 4-4).

Reward

Candice works efficiently and produces the best results when she knows what's in it for her. If you put her on a team with cowork-

Table 4-4. High need for security

Common Tugs	Common Shoves
Contracts History (few layoffs, low turnover, etc.) Clear job role and duties	Risk Rapid change

ers who don't pull their load but will get the same reward, her motivation decreases rapidly.

Employees like Candice, who have a high need for reward, are looking for the tangibles they can accumulate through their work. They want to know how much they can earn and how they can earn it. They want to know how they will be compensated for their time and effort. And they need to have it spelled out clearly. High-reward people like to see that effort and compensation are clearly aligned. They typically do not like systems that reward time in a job over effort in a job (see Table 4-5).

Table 4-5. High need for reward

Common Tugs	Common Shoves
Pay for performance Incentives Perks Praise Recognition	Pay for time Low performers with same pay

Adventure

Christine is easily bored. She's an adrenaline junkie and needs to do interesting and cutting-edge work. If there's a new or experimental project, she's all over it. She doesn't much care for stupid people and thus often works by herself. Give her a risky project with lots of autonomy, and she's ecstatic. Put her with a large group of mediocre minds doing boring work, and she's ready to take a header off her cubicle wall.

People like Christine have a need for adventure and are motivated by risk, change, and uncertainty. They thrive when the environment or the work is constantly changing. They tend to like challenges and jump at the opportunity to be the first to do something new. They don't mind failure, especially if given the chance to try again. High-adventure people often go out on their own. They may be entrepreneurs or freelancers. They are likely to change jobs and companies often, especially when they get bored or feel that they have maxed out their potential somewhere (see Table 4-6).

Table 4-6. High need for adventure

Common Tugs	Common Shoves
Difficult tasks New tasks and jobs Change Being "the first"	Repetitive tasks and jobs Easy or simple tasks and jobs

Actualization

Bill is driven by a need to feel good about himself and the work he does. Last month he worked on a project that developed creative ways to increase teaching about healthy living and eating in the public school system, and he was more driven and productive than he'd ever been.

Folks like Bill, who have a need for actualization, focus on a desire for self-fulfillment, namely the tendency to reach their own greatest potential. They want to maximize themselves in the world through their job. High-actualization people tend to concentrate more on their own goals than on the goals of a company—although those goals can be aligned (see Table 4-7).

Table 4-7. High need for actualization

Common Tugs	Common Shoves
Setting own goals Focusing on personal growth Looking at how current job fits with future plans Participating in continuing education, seminars, etc.	Lack of opportunities for personal growth Micromanagement

It's critical that when you pitch anything important to your people, you gear it directly to the individual needs of the type of person you're dealing with. Your actualization people probably aren't looking for a whole lot of power, nor will your reward people be overly interested in the social connections your affiliation people want. Your security-focused people will not want the adventure angle (and vice versa). People driven by security don't want to hear what an exciting risk this is and how no one in the industry has ever before attempted this kind of move. Adventure people don't want to hear how proven the concept is (they want to be on the cutting edge). And so on. The real key is to listen carefully to your Shoves and Tugs conversations and then, coupled with what you now know about these common personality types, frame your solutions in a way that's tailored to the person sitting in front of you.

Taking Action

As you meet with each employee, make a clear list of that person's Shoves and Tugs. A simple line down the middle of the page with Shoves listed on one side and Tugs on the other is all you need. First, look at the Shoves, the issues that need fixing. If it appears that getting rid of a Shove will have a positive return on investment (ROI) and deliver you a Hundred Percenter, then you want to do whatever it takes (within reason, of course) to eliminate or neutralize the Shove—before you even think about granting any Tugs. Remember, you have to stop hitting their toes with the hammer before they can enjoy the back rub.

By the way, notwithstanding that you're going to hear different answers from every employee, you may start to identify some themes. If there are Shoves that are endemic to you as a leader, or to your department or even your organization, you may hear those. In fact, this can sometimes feel like a real-time 360° assessment. You will likely hear how your natural leadership tendencies are being received (e.g., you like to be in control, but are you coming off as a micromanager?), and you'll have sufficient feedback to tell you if you need to make some adjustments.

Once you've eliminated the critical Shoves, take the same approach with the Tugs. Find issues you can tackle that have a positive ROI, and just get going. And while you do it, keep in mind which of the seven personality types you are dealing with, and address them with the kind of words and actions they want to see and hear.

Putting It Together

Because the Shoves and Tugs that every leader will face are going to be significantly different, I can't supply you with a one-size-fits-all motivator. However, what I can do is show you how Leo, the director of marketing for StayHealthyInc., addressed the Shoves and Tugs of all seven of the employees we visited with earlier. First, Leo mapped out each employee's Shoves and Tugs and then came up with individual action plans. Let's take a look.

Grace

Leo first met with Grace, who, as you may recall, has a high need for achievement. They met casually over coffee, and Grace was eager to respond when Leo asked her about the motivators and demotivators she had experienced during the past month or two.

"I'm really glad you asked that Leo, because I can't help but feel that some of the work I'm doing isn't going to help us hit those HARD goals you set last month.

"Like that proposal I gave you last month. We could be driving so much more traffic to the Web site if we had an upgraded virtual shopping system. I know memberships are our key focus, and they bring in a lot of revenue, but we've got some great products that rival the competition. Only no one knows about them. I know how to turn this around; I just need the chance to prove it."

Grace was committed to giving Leo the information he was after. Because she's a good employee with a strong work ethic, she's not likely to ask for something as unreasonable as being released from all menial tasks in order to chase wild and unpredictable chances. However, she did let Leo know she'd like a little more time to focus on more challenging work. And because Leo is familiar with the seven driving needs and because he recognizes Grace as having a personality type that is focused on achievement, he was able gain a deeper appreciation of their conversation.

After giving the situation some thought, Leo again met with Grace to discuss what he could do regarding her Shoves and Tugs.

"I reread your proposal, Grace, and I agree that while some of it is risky, the payoff could be worthwhile and help us hit our HARD goals. Now, I do still need you on the budget work and the internal assignments. However, I potentially could do something to open up about 15 to 20% of your time, given that your other work stays consistently strong. I read that Google has a thing it calls 20% time where employees can work on projects like this that they're passionate about, so I'm willing to try it.

"I'm not saying your proposal will automatically fly and you've got free rein. I need to see some big preliminary results before I can bring this before my boss. So how about this: I'll give you three months with some focused time on this project. I'm going to need weekly progress meetings, and we'll need to see adequate progress. After three months, if you're meeting the criteria that you and I will lay out together, I'll get you a meeting with the folks who have the power to approve the next steps. I still need you to pull the same load around here, but I'll give you a chance to make this happen."

Sue

The next day, Leo met with Sue, who likes to have power and control. When Leo asked Sue about her Shoves and Tugs, she was not quite as forthcoming as was Grace.

"I don't know, Leo. I mean, it's all part of the job. What's this about anyway? Is there something going on I need to know about?"

Sue was suspicious of Leo's intentions and leery of revealing her thoughts in case it got her in trouble. Despite Leo's reassurance that there would be no negative repercussions, Sue stayed tight-lipped. Leo chatted pleasantly for five minutes and then called a friendly halt to the meeting. He decided it would be best for Sue to observe how he addressed other employees' Shoves and Tugs over the next few weeks. He hoped it would encourage her to open up the next time they met.

When they met in a month, Sue, while still a bit hesitant, was more open to talking.

"I don't mean this with any disrespect, Leo, and I'm hesitant to even say anything. But sometimes I feel just a little too monitored, like you don't think I can do the job. And if that's the case, I'd like it if you would tell me. You said you believed that I could hit those HARD goals, even though they're really hard, and I believed you. The thing is that I've got dreams of being a manager one day. I think I have real strengths in leadership, and I'd like the opportunity to develop those skills. I love this company, and I'd like to hang in for the long run. Only I need some kind of reassurance that my hard work is going to take me where I want to go."

Leo felt a bit ruffled when Sue implied that he was a micro-manager. But he kept things in perspective and was able to see that, due to Sue's penchant for power, it might actually behoove him, and push Sue to greater performance, if he were to pull back a bit when it came to managing her. He's hopeful that with a little less monitoring she will start to produce the Hundred Percenter effort he knows she's capable of.

Sue isn't the only employee Leo manages who has dreams of leadership, but out of all of them, she shows the most promise. There's nothing Leo could have done at that moment to give Sue the kind of power and visibility she craves, so he didn't lie to her. But he let her know he will put her in a leadership role for the very next team effort, which is coming up next month. And if she proves herself there, there will be recurring leadership roles.

Rory

Next, Leo met with Rory, who gravitates toward affiliation. He's the guy who likes everyone and wants to be liked back. Given his personality type, Rory was a little hesitant to tell Leo anything that might sound harsh or cause waves. Because Leo understands Rory's driving needs, he quickly turned his line of Shoves and Tugs questioning to a third-party focus, allowing Rory to speak his mind under the guise of bringing benefit to the whole team. That was all it took to get Rory talking.

"I know I'm not the only one who sometimes feels isolated in my work. And I think for us to hit our HARD goals, less isolation would be really beneficial. I've talked to a lot of people who want more teamwork as we're working on these goals. I heard about this idea called a No Homework Team. It's where you get everyone together in a meeting, and you fix the problem right there with everyone's help. You know, different from how we normally do it, where we all take our little piece and meet up again in a couple of days to put it all together. I think it would really bring an enhanced level of teamwork to the company."

Leo has a special interest in addressing Rory's Shoves and Tugs. Not only is Rory a talented employee who has great potential to reach Hundred Percenter status, he's also an influencer. Everyone in the office looks to him for guidance. Leo knows that kind of power can go a long way in getting folks to see the benefit in giving Hundred Percenter performance. If Rory gives the thumbs-up, Leo's job becomes infinitely easier.

Luckily, Rory isn't asking for anything over the top, as is typically the case. Hundred Percenters, or those with potential to be such, will rarely overstep the bounds when asked about Shoves and Tugs.

After listening to what Rory had to say, Leo immediately responded.

"I could see where a No Homework Team could be effective. I'll tell you what, Rory. We've got a team meeting scheduled for next week. I'll try the No Homework approach if you're willing to put together the agenda and teach us how to make it happen. If it goes smoothly and you can show me some solid evidence to back the results, we'll try it again. Then you and I will sit down and measure the effectiveness of this approach and how and when it best fits our needs. I can't promise you every meeting is going to be like this, but if it brings results, yeah, I'm willing to give it a go."

Paul

Paul is all about security and no-risk assurance of success. When he sat down with Leo, he was definitely on the borderline of superficial and suspicious when it came to talking about his Shoves and Tugs.

"Everything's fine, Leo. I have no complaints. I'm really happy here."

Rather than push the issue and make Paul shut down more, Leo encouraged him to talk about his Shoves and Tugs in the third person. "Then maybe you can tell me a few things you think other employees like and dislike about the organization." Paul remained hesitant, but he did open up a little.

"Well, I have heard a few things. You know, like we're wasting a lot of time doing work that isn't going to help us hit the department's HARD goals."

This didn't give Leo a whole lot to go on, and so he pushed Paul to divulge more information. "Can you give me some examples of this, Paul?"

"Well, I know last month when we were working on strengthening the brand image, it was really hectic. A bunch of us put in a lot of overtime, often doing stuff that wasn't really productive but that I suppose needed to get done. But it got really stressful."

Leo nodded his head and said, "This is good for me to know, Paul. Look, you're in there working with everyone. Do you have any ideas for how we can make things better?"

"Yeah, actually I do. Part of what's killing us is the rush to produce the Monthly Analytics report. We need the report, but the way we have to rush it out for that crazy deadline every month means we're wasting huge time waiting for other areas because they don't have their data finished. And then, because they aren't on time with their data, the data aren't entered into the central database, which means the whole process is totally manual, which is a killer. And the worst part? The executives don't even read the report until 2 weeks later at their Executive Roundtable meeting. One of the guys in IT told me that if we waited 1 extra week until all the data were loaded, the report would take 30 minutes to produce rather than 2 weeks, and we'd have it done in plenty of time for the executives' meeting. You wanna know what really keeps me up at night? The whole report is so rushed and manual and cobbled together, I'm in a cold sweat that the numbers are wrong."

Leo was learning that once you get folks talking, not only will they tell you their Shoves and Tugs, but they'll outline the exact steps necessary to fix them. Leo asked Paul, "Are you willing to do a little work to discover why that arbitrary deadline was originally set that way? And are you willing to write up everything you just said into a couple of paragraphs so we can try to fix this process, which seems really broken?" Paul's eyes lit up when he replied, "Seriously, honest-to-goodness process improvement? Consistency, predictably, and accuracy? Man, I'm all over that."

It took a little time conversing, but Leo was able to get Paul not only to admit what was shoving him into unhappiness, but to volunteer what would tug him toward greater performance. Even better, Paul was willing to do the legwork to make his Tug a reality.

Candice

Candice is inspired to work hard when she knows there is a tangible reward. She's already seen Leo's efforts in action to address her coworkers' Shoves and Tugs and is all too happy to talk to Leo.

"I'm so glad it's finally my turn. I think it's great you're doing this, and I love that I finally have a boss who cares. I know you sort of kicked us in the rear a bit with those new HARD goals, but I appreciate that we're aiming for something really worth hitting. The thing I want to talk to you about is my performance on hitting those goals. I'm really trying, but I constantly feel like I'm missing the mark. I don't think I really understand the measurements for our pay-for-performance program. Last month I handled that huge problem with our biggest vendor and did the kickoff for five new gyms, but I didn't see anything for my efforts. I'm really confused."

While it may seem that Candice is only out for what she can get, Leo knows that her reward-motivated personality gets jump-started by the promise of compensation. And while Leo isn't about to hand her something for nothing, he quickly sees a way to turn Candice's admission about her Shoves and Tugs into a strategy for pushing her to Hundred Percenter performance.

"I think it's great you want to aim higher, Candice, and I'm happy to help. I think we can start solving this. What do you say we meet tomorrow, for about 30 minutes, and really dig into the measures in the performance plan and look at where you've been at for the past few months. Let's make sure everything is clear, and we can talk about any parts that don't make sense. We'll come up with a few goals and some strategies to achieve them, and we'll give you the next week to see what you can do. Then we'll meet again next week and compare notes. You tell me what it was like, and I'll give you my feedback on what I saw. Together, I feel confident we can get you on track to where you want to go and in the right direction of our HARD goals."

Christine

Christine seeks adventure and hits Hundred Percenter performance when her adrenalin is running strong. The Shoves and Tugs she set before Leo didn't surprise him at all.

"Some of the work is really repetitive, and while I understand it has to get done, I just wish once in a while there was something more. It would make the menial stuff more tolerable. I don't want to come off sounding like a complainer, because I am really happy. I just want some bigger challenges, and I'd really like to be involved in some of the really tough parts of the HARD goals."

Leo understands that adventure and change is what drives Christine to achieve. He admits that it's been a while since he gave her anything to really sate her appetite, and he realizes he could potentially lose a valuable employee if he doesn't do something soon to address her Shoves. The good news is that the HARD goals they've set now offer opportunities aplenty for this adventurous spirit. He has a task team he's putting together, and he offers Christine the challenge of leading it. He makes it clear that the job comes with very tough targets, but he knows with Christine, the harder he pushes, the more she'll achieve.

Bill

Finally, Leo met with Bill, who is driven by actualization, a need to keep growing. Bill had heard from the others about how these meetings were going down, and so he was prepared to talk about his Shoves and Tugs.

"The thing is, Leo, I feel kind of lost. I like the job, but I just don't feel any sense of direction or where I'm going with it all. Lately it's like I show up, do my work, and go home. I'm just not learning anything; my brain's kind of atrophying."

Leo knows it's to his advantage to help Bill chart out his future and recognize the opportunities where he can really push himself to grow and develop.

"I can understand your frustration, Bill, and I can definitely help you find your way. These new HARD goals are going to require us to learn some things we don't presently know how to do. I've got some projects I think will stretch your brain. I'd welcome the chance to meet with you and discuss them. I could do it as soon as tomorrow, say one o'clock; we'll we meet for an hour and start to map out a plan to really stretch you."

Conclusion

In sum, maximizing the Tugs and minimizing the Shoves keeps employees tied to their organization, committed to Hundred Percenter performance, and dedicated to achieving your HARD goals. Each person has his or her unique Shoves and Tugs, and these Shoves and Tugs are not static. What StayHealthyInc. has shown us is that "one size fits one" and that, like our waistlines over the years, sizes are always changing.

5

100% Skills with 0% Attitude

There's one group of employees who present a unique set of challenges to making your HARD goals happen. We call them Talented Terrors. They're the employees who have the skills you want but the attitudes you don't want. Most leaders admit that managing an employee with a bad attitude is difficult, but they stop short when it comes to labeling Talented Terrors as low performers. "You mean Jim in Accounting? I'll admit that he doesn't do anything without an argument first. But that's just who he is. Besides, he's got talent. He may have a lousy attitude, but he's still got what it takes to be a high performer."

Well, some people may feel Jim is a high performer, but this is a point with which 100% Leaders strongly disagree. They know that no matter how skilled an employee may be, if a bad attitude is part of the package, that person is not a Hundred Percenter, and there are no exceptions to the rule. HARD goals aren't achieved by Hundred Percenter skill alone. They also require the Hundred

Percenter attitude. The employees of ChocoBot may have all the technical knowledge needed to achieve the HARD goal set before them. But just one person who grumbles and groans at the prospect of doing the work can stand in the way seeing that goal realized.

If you think I'm exaggerating the Talented Terror factor just for impact, we've got a substantial study that backs our convictions. Leadership IQ conducted a three-year hiring study that tracked 5,000 leaders who collectively hired over 20,000 employees. Like most organizations, the ones we studied typically interviewed and hired for skill. The candidate review process focused primarily on "What can you do and how well can you do it?"

The results of this study are significant to every facet of leadership, not just hiring. We learned that 46% of new hires fail within 18 months of starting the job. Unsettling to hear, but here's the part that's really critical: out of the 46% of employees who fail to become any kind of acceptable performer, let alone Hundred Percenters, only 11% of the time a lack of technical ability, or skill, is to blame. For the other 89% of the time, a lousy attitude is the clear reason behind employee failure.

This is certainly great information to have. But we took our study a step further and found out exactly what it is that defines the bad attitude that makes these folks such poor performers.

Failure due to lack of coachability, 26%. Employees don't accept and implement feedback from bosses, colleagues, customers, and others.

Failure due to poor emotional intelligence, 23%. Employees lack the ability to understand and manage their own emotions and to accurately assess others' emotions.

Failure due to lack of motivation, 17%. Employees lack the positive attitudes that fuel the drive to achieve their full potential and to excel at the job.

Failure due to the wrong temperament, 15%. Employees have the wrong attitude and personality for a particular job and work environment.

This should certainly make you rethink the focus of your hiring practices. But it also shows that unequivocally, no matter how skilled an employee may be, if there's a lousy attitude at play, especially one that involves lack of coachability, poor emotional intelligence, lack of motivation, and the wrong temperament, you're not looking at Hundred Percenter material. That is, unless you get the employee to willingly readjust his or her bad attitude—which, in a good number of cases, is not all that difficult to do.

Bottom line, if you want to bring your HARD goals to life, Talented Terrors have to be turned around. But doing so presents some unique leadership challenges. If an employee lacks skill, there's usually a clear-cut way to define the problem and demand a change: "John, the monthly reports are three days late, and I found nine errors. Let's review the specifics and what you can do to fix this . . ." It's also fairly easy to correct a lack of skill. In this case, you could try giving John more detailed instructions or even get him some extra training.

But how do you definitively prove a bad attitude such as pessimism, sarcasm, inflexibility, or surliness? A statement like, "John, your comments in last week's meeting were rude and really brought down the team," sounds pretty subjective. What's more, it can easily be deflected with a clever comeback (and, boy, are Talented Terrors clever) like, "Gee, I was only doing what you asked from the team by expressing my viewpoint. I was just following your leadership."

Make no mistake. Talented Terrors have been playing the bad-attitude game for a long time—probably far longer than you've been at the leadership game. They're smart, often even as smart as you, and they know how to twist the facts and turn the blame. And even if you do manage to keep the focus of a conversation on the bad attitude, there's an even bigger challenge to face: how do you turn a bad attitude into a Hundred Percenter attitude?

We decided to take on the challenge and turn the Talented Terror problem around. Our first step was to go to the front lines and evaluate the situation. We conducted several well-known studies of leaders and Talented Terrors from a wide variety of industries. Our goal was to put skilled people with bad attitudes under the microscope and to learn what works and what doesn't work when it comes to showing these folks the way to the Hundred Percenter path.

We learned it's more than possible to turn Talented Terrors around, but it takes a bit of tough love; not a task every leader relishes. However, tolerating Talented Terrors isn't an option. And here are the reasons why.

Why Attitude Matters

Let's say you have a programmer on your team who has written more code than anyone else on earth, and his skill has gotten you out of a few jams. Even so, you privately think the guy's a jerk, and he's making your life miserable. He comes in late and leaves early, all the while giving you a look that says, "Dare and call me on this, and I won't be there for you next time you need me." He's got a permanent scowl plastered on his face, and he seems to get a real thrill from challenging authority, especially yours, and usually when his peers are watching. In other words, you've got a Talented Terror on your hands.

It drives you crazy, but you let it ride because you know this person has tremendous skill. When he does let loose with a burst of aptitude, seemingly just when you need it most, amazing things happen. Sure, his bad attitude is frustrating, and sometimes downright annoying to deal with, but does it really warrant any action on your part? After all, beyond your own annoyance, how much damage can this person actually do?

The answer is plenty, as in plenty of damage, because there's no such thing as a Hundred Percenter with bad attitude. Attitude matters. I've already made the case linking bad attitude and lousy performance, but there are three more ways that Talented Terrors can do damage to an organization and destroy HARD goals.

1. Talented Terrors Negatively Impact the Team

Talented Terrors are like the bully back in high school. They wield a lot of power for all the wrong reasons. Some employees may be intimidated by the Talented Terror, some may worship him, and others may think he's a pain in the butt who creates problems and slows down productivity. But you probably don't have too many people who are prepared to take on the Talented Terror. Workplace politics are complex, and it's simply easier to try and stay under the bully's radar. Only that's the last thing Talented Terrors want. Misery loves company, and they'll do everything they can to drag the rest of the team down to their level.

Hundred Percenters and other good employees may tolerate Talented Terrors in order to make life easier, but they don't like it. In fact, it makes them miserable. Your best people want to work in an upbeat and productive environment where every team member is valuable and pulling his or her own weight. Hundred Percenters and Hundred Percenters in the making aren't going to stick around very long if they are forced to exist in a culture where a bad attitude is tolerated by the boss. Or if they do, chances are they'll eventually succumb to the negative pressure.

"Not my employees," you may be thinking. "My folks are smarter than that." This would be nice if it were true, but it's not. We conducted a survey of more than 70,000 employees. One question we asked of the Hundred Percenters was, "What's it like to work with folks who have a lousy attitude?" A whopping 87% said Talented Terror coworkers make them so miserable that they have seriously considered changing jobs. To darken the picture even further, an even higher 93% admitted their productivity level dropped when forced to work alongside Talented Terrors.

If you've got Talented Terrors on your team, it's almost certain the whole team is suffering because of them. What's more, your Hundred Percenters, the ones you absolutely don't want to lose, may be making plans for the future that don't include working for you. And that's not going to do anything to help your HARD goals happen.

We know these numbers are high, and so we invite you to reaffirm our study findings by conducting an impromptu survey of your own. Go out into your front lines and talk to your best people. They don't have to be Hundred Percenters yet—just the folks who have both the skills and the attitude that come close to what you ideally want. Ask them the following question: "Would you rather work with a low-performing coworker with a bad attitude or work short staffed?" We guarantee the answer will be, "I'd rather work short staffed."

Your best employees may thrive on hard work, but as much as they may love the challenge, they still have the hardest job in the organization. Remember, when it's late Friday afternoon and a proposal has to be written by Monday in order to retain a multimillion dollar client, it's not the folks with the bad attitudes who give up their weekends to make sure the job gets done. It's your Hundred Percenters.

Just ask Alexa. A valuable member of a marketing team for a well-known line of sporting goods, she's been with the organization for almost six years. Alexa loves her job, is good at what she does, and feels a strong sense of loyalty toward the company. She has all the earmarks of a Hundred Percenter. That is, until about six months ago, around the time her coworker Lydia was hired. Ever since Lydia came on board, Alexa's life has been a living hell, and it's starting to show in her work.

Lydia last worked for a big East Coast competitor. She's got a knack for throwing out innovative ideas during brainstorming sessions, and she has introduced some new and much-needed technology to the organization. Some people are really excited about her potential talent, especially the boss, Greg. This has Alexa wondering if Greg isn't selectively blind and deaf. Granted, Lydia has some exceptional skills, but she's also got an incredibly bad attitude. Alexa is baffled about why Greg seems to overlook this fact.

Take this past week, for example. On Monday, Lydia was given an assignment to complete a report as part of a HARD goal that had a strict Friday deadline. She accepted the task with a smile, but as soon as she was out of Greg's auditory range, she told Alexa how she really felt. "This stupid goal of his will never fly," she said. "It's unrealistic. Besides, I would never have been asked to do anything like this at my old job."

The next day the report remained untouched, and Lydia still had plenty to say. "I still can't believe Greg thinks this goal is a good idea," she said. "There's no way we get paid enough to do this kind of work. We're better than this. Do you realize how much more other organizations are paying? And at least their employees are appreciated. When's the last time Greg did anything to show you he's thankful for the hard work you do?"

As the week progressed, Alexa continued to be on the receiving end of Lydia's grumbling about the project and her feelings of disdain for Greg, the company, her coworkers, and the client. Alexa felt drained from listening to it, but she had to admit, Lydia's chronic complaining had piqued her interest about what other opportunities might be out there.

Alexa also had some serious concerns about the report; had it even been started? There were a lot of people waiting to get those results. She got her answer on Friday, just after lunch. Upon returning to the office, she saw Lydia crumpled at her desk tearfully talking to Greg. "I tried to get it done. I really did," Lydia said. "But with no support from the rest of the team, and all the other work I have . . . well, and the client refused to cooperate."

As Greg turned her way, Alexa knew what was coming. She picked up the phone to call her husband and let him know their dinner plans were off. Once again, it would be a late night at the office scrambling to finish Lydia's work.

If you want to know what it's like for your employees to work with a Talented Terror, stop for a minute and put yourself in Alexa's shoes, or those of your own high or middle performers. Given the choice, would you pick getting dragged through an emotional circus and being stuck at the office until midnight on a Friday doing someone else's work? Or would you opt for getting rid of the person with the bad attitude and just dealing with the extra work on your own time and without all the drama? Or would you perhaps even think about checking out and finding a job where everyone has a great attitude and gets the work done?

The only way to hold on to your Hundred Percenters and inspire others to rise to the same is to make it clear—with no exceptions—that in your organization, a bad attitude isn't an option.

2. Talented Terrors Destroy Leadership Effectiveness

Talented Terrors can also impact how your team evaluates and respects your leadership capabilities. And it goes far deeper than the verbal slamming these bullies may give you behind your back. The way you choose to manage Talented Terrors sends a message to the rest of your people—a message that can deliver a home run to your HARD goal or send it into foul territory before it even reaches first base.

Tolerating a bad attitude from even a single employee sends the following message to your best people: "Go ahead and underperform all you want; we encourage that here. We don't care how much you complain or drag your feet; you're guaranteed the same respect and benefits as the folks who have a great attitude and are getting the work done right."

And if that isn't enough to completely discourage your Hundred Percenters, there's also the factor of your time and how you choose to use it. Of the leaders we surveyed, 93% said they spend significantly more time with their low performers than they do with their middle or high performers. That sends a pretty strong message to your best people about where your priorities are.

Let's go back to Alexa and Lydia to see how this can play out. Greg, their boss, knows he can depend on Alexa to do a great job and get it done on time. However, Lydia is another story. It's obvious from the work she has completed that she's got skills. But more often than not, Lydia fails to meet her deadlines, always with a lengthy excuse and a fair amount of drama.

In response, Greg has started devoting more and more of his time to helping Lydia stay on track. He meets with her each day to oversee and monitor her assignments. And when things go wrong, as they inevitably do, it takes a good chunk of his time to work around Lydia's defensiveness to let her know why her work is incomplete or incorrect. Greg is hopeful that this dedication of time will pay off and that Lydia will work past her bad attitude and become the Hundred Percenter he thinks she can be.

Of course, this means Greg has little to no time to focus on Alexa or any of his other high performers. Five months ago, at Alexa's last performance review, Greg promised her some extra training that could lead to a promotion. But dealing with Lydia is taking up all his extra time. Greg hasn't spoken to Alexa about it, but he feels certain she understands what's going on. Once he gets Lydia up to speed, he has every intention of turning his focus toward getting Alexa the training she deserves.

Unfortunately, Alexa's interpretation of the situation isn't what Greg thinks it is. She tried giving Greg the benefit of the doubt, but she's starting to think Lydia might be right, that maybe all this hard work isn't worth it. Besides, when was the last time Greg did or said anything to show his appreciation? An empty promise about a promotion is even worse than doing nothing at all.

Alexa is bent out of shape, and while she's not typically someone who spreads gossip, she is so upset that she's started expressing her discontent to a few of her trusted and talented peers. "I just don't understand all the time Greg lavishes on Lydia," she confided in one coworker. "It's like a slap in the face for all the hard work we contribute to the organization. Where is our incentive to reach this HARD goal he threw our way? I'm starting to question Greg's abilities as a leader and wonder whether there's any real value in working so hard. I was promised training and a possible promotion that has obviously been forgotten. We might as well stop giving so much effort and just cop a lousy attitude. Greg doesn't seem to notice, and it sure seems to be working for Lydia."

Not only is Alexa losing faith in Greg's ability to lead, but she's also starting to think it might be worth her while to become a Talented Terror. And as long as Greg continues to tolerate Lydia's bad attitude, he'll only strengthen Alexa's conviction that giving less is a better way to go.

3. Talented Terrors Get Leaders Fired

If you're still not convinced that managing Talented Terrors is a priority, here's something that should get your full attention: they can cost you your job. For one of our most famous studies (on why CEOs get fired), we interviewed just over 1,000 board members from 286 public, private, business, and health-care organizations in a four-year study that looked at why these organizations fired, or otherwise forced out, their chief executives. Tolerating low performers, which Talented Terrors most definitely are, was the number three reason for termination.

As the example with Alexa and Lydia shows, when leaders fail to make an effort to improve or discipline Talented Terrors, it destroys their leadership credibility and makes it politically difficult for them to hold other employees accountable. We know Lydia's bad attitude is having a negative impact on Alexa, and likely anyone else whose ear Lydia can grab and complain in, but it goes even deeper than that.

Alexa is one of the organization's most valuable high performers, and as such, she wields her own power in the workplace, usually to generate positive motivation. But lately she's been sharing her feelings of unhappiness, and folks are taking note. If Alexa is questioning whether the extra effort to bring about a HARD goal is worth it, other employees will soon start to do the same. Lydia's bad attitude combined with Alexa's discontent is almost guaranteed to create an epidemic of bad attitude and lack of commitment to HARD goals. As a result, there are going to be obvious and undesirable changes in overall performance results. And this is something Greg's superiors are sure to notice, and take action on.

Parenthetically, we did a series of experiments in which we assessed the moods of employees who attended team meetings together. We found that when a group had a few really upbeat people—without any really negative people—the overall mood of the group improved slightly over the course of a one- to two-hour meeting. That is, positive people had a slight positive impact on those around them. But when the group had even one significantly negative person, the mood of the whole group decreased significantly within a one- to two-hour meeting. This was true even if there were significantly positive people in the group as well. The lesson? Bad moods are much more infectious than positive moods. Have you seen the bumper sticker that says "Smiles are contagious?" According to our research, it should be changed to read "Frowns are contagious, so avoid negative people."

The facts are in: a talented employee with a bad attitude is far more than an inconvenience. Talented Terrors are real trouble, and it only makes sense to do something to turn the problem around. Yet we've found that only 14% of senior executives think their companies are doing a good job at managing these low performers. And only 17% of middle managers say they feel comfortable taking action to improve or terminate Talented Terrors. In the face of the overwhelming evidence of the damage that Talented Terrors can do, we are forced to ask, why aren't more leaders doing something about it?

Why Bad Attitude Goes Unchecked

If your organization is like most, it's not difficult to figure out why Talented Terrors are allowed to go unchecked. Just take a look at the current company standards you use to evaluate employee performance. The criteria most leaders depend upon are skill based. But we now know that aptitude factors such as knowledge of work and the quantity and quality of that work are responsible for only 11% of employee failure. Attitude, not skill, is often the primary differentiator of Hundred Percenter performance.

But even performance reviews that incorporate an attitude assessment can fail to identify Talented Terrors. That's because the high skill ratings these folks score create a halo effect that distorts the truth about their lousy attitude. So there are a lot of Talented Terrors out there who are regularly being reviewed and rewarded for their bad attitude—in spite of all the damage they do. This only feeds their fire and motivates them to continue the bad behavior.

What's more, Talented Terrors are really good actors. They don't want to get nabbed by the wrong person, and so they become brilliant at turning their bad attitude on and off as it benefits them. You may have an employee who is your worst nightmare, but when the CEO of the company walks by, you can bet that employee will be on the mark with a winning attitude. "Good morning, Mr. Jones. Great news about the shareholder's meeting. I just can't wait to get started on these new initiatives. In fact, I stayed up late last night so I could give my boss a few ideas on how we might reduce costs. Well, I better get back to work—great to see you, and make sure to give your wife my best."

With so much focus on skill, and some pretty incredible theatrical performances taking place, it's easy to see how a toxic attitude can slip beneath the radar. The boss or the boss's boss may only see the work produced and not the damage being done. And when a Hundred Percenter quits because he or she is sick and tired of working with a Talented Terror, unless that fact comes out during the exit interview, and it rarely does, no one ever learns the truth.

What About Employees Who Refuse to Change?

Many Talented Terrors will change when presented with the techniques we're about to show you. But there are some who won't. The good news is that for the folks who refuse to change, our typical results show that 60% of incurable low performers will voluntarily choose to quit when presented with the "Improve or Remove" tactics below. This eliminates the dirty work and legal snafus of having to fire these people. And let's face it; too many leaders will do almost anything to avoid the stress of terminating an employee, no matter how poor the person's performance.

Now let's take a look at the Improve or Remove leadership techniques that can help you turn your Talented Terrors into the Hundred Percenters you want.

Managing Bad Attitudes

The next time you see and hear a child throwing a tantrum in the supermarket aisle, fight the urge to flee and, instead, go in for a closer look. How are the parents responding? If they are racing to indulge the little terror in whatever he or she wants, there's a good chance you're witnessing a Talented Terror in the making.

Undesirable attitudes like negativity, narcissism, reluctance, gossiping, and instigating didn't just pop into existence the day these folks came to work for you. The first signs of a bad attitude generally emerge between the ages of 2 and 10. So by the time a Talented Terror walks through the doors of your organization 10, 20, or 30 years later, that person's had a lot of time to perfect his or her act. And if that person's parents, teachers, spiritual counselors, therapists, etc., haven't succeeded in fixing the underlying personality issues by now, you're probably not going to either.

The critical mistake most leaders make in attempting to manage a bad attitude is taking a therapeutic approach. Given the day-to-day demands of the workplace, most leaders, even if they have the clinical training to do so, don't have the time and energy to take on the job of restructuring an employee's personality. Quite honestly, that's a job many qualified psychologists are even reluctant to handle. But that doesn't mean the situation is hopeless. In many cases, you can't fix the underlying personality that drives a bad attitude, but you can put a stop to the behavioral manifestations of the bad attitude.

There are six rules for managing the behaviors that accompany a bad attitude:

1. Timeliness
2. Objectivity
3. Specificity
4. Candor
5. Calm
6. Choice

First, we are going to explore each rule on its own to see how it works. Then we'll show you how to combine all six rules into a simple script that can be used to diffuse even the most undesirable behaviors.

Timeliness

Paul loves his job as the manager of a home improvement retail store. The customers are great, and he's got a team of Hundred Percenters that regularly bring good results, with the exception of one employee. It's not that the employee, Darren, lacks skill. In fact, he knows home improvement better than anyone else. The problem is Darren's attitude. He's confrontational with coworkers and has been heard expressing negative comments about the company to customers. And when Paul recently gave the team a HARD goal, Darren made it loudly known that he had no intention of doing anything that fell outside his job description.

Paul has put up with Darren's lousy attitude until now due to his skills. But enough customer and coworker complaints have been registered to make it clear that Darren's bad attitude is hurting the organization more than his skills are helping it. Over the past months, Paul has kept a written ledger of Darren's attitudinal problems, jotting each one down as it happens. When it came time for Darren's yearly review, Paul felt fully prepared to confront him about his bad attitude. Only the review didn't go as planned. As Paul read off his list, his anger started to build as he realized just how many times Darren had stepped outside of bounds and let his bad attitude hurt the organization.

In an effort to keep his cool, Paul quickly changed his tactic. He put the list down and said, "Look, Darren, I could go on reading this list, but the point here is that your attitude is lousy. You represent the company in a negative light to customers, you criticize your coworkers, and you have no respect for the authority I hold as manager. Your bad attitude is weighing heavily on this organization, and I need it to stop immediately."

Darren didn't miss a beat. He also was prepared for the meeting. "I'm curious why none of this comes up when you need my expertise," he said. "Like six months ago, when no one but me could help the customer with all the roofing questions? And how about the time I helped Andy over in paints? Remember that? The wrong shipment came in, and someone shelved the whole thing. I was the one who volunteered to stay late and help sort it out. And how about when you asked me to help out in electronics during the holiday season? I got right to work without any argument even though it isn't my department. So how can you say I don't respect your leadership?"

Paul found out the hard way that you can't let an attitude problem build over time and then expect to drop the hammer on it and fix the behavior during a yearly review. Talented Terrors are smart, and they stockpile every positive performance example they can get their hands on for when they finally do get called to task. Paul may be focused on the last 10 times Darren came in late, but Darren is going to be way ahead of him. He's got a list of his own, of all the things he's done right; a list that weakens Paul's argument and makes it look overblown and irrational. And while Paul's accumulated irritation reaches its peak, Darren is feeling calmer and more in control as he savors every moment of watching Paul's frustration build.

You need to confront the issues with Talented Terrors as they happen. Putting off until tomorrow what you can fix today is one of the major flaws of yearly employee reviews. And most HARD goals won't survive if resistance is tolerated for any length of time. Besides, how many times of doing something wrong does it take to make it significant? If the Navy SEALs are launching a mission at 0600 hours and Chuck lumbers in at 0615 and says, "Sorry, dude, but I had a late night," what do you think is going to happen? Or if a surgeon forgets to perform a critical procedure because he's in a rush to make a lunch date, is it excusable if he kills only one patient? Your circumstances may not be quite as life or death as these, but you still don't have to wait until something really terrible happens before you do something about a Talented Terror.

It may have been the straw that broke the camel's back, but there were a whole lot of straws that got piled on before the collapse actually happened. Don't let a series of bad situations pile up until you reach your final straw. The best way to deliver feedback about a bad attitude is in real time. That means no more than 48 hours after the incident you are addressing. Not only will the facts be fresh, thus more difficult for the employee to dodge, but you won't be coming from the dangerous place of accumulated anger.

Objectivity

Talented Terrors are like anyone else when it comes to receiving bad news; they would rather not hear it. If they hear negative words like "angry," "disgusted," "annoyed," "unsupported," "deceived," "abused," "controlled," "punished," "wronged," "tricked," or "used," chances are good they are going to check out of the conversation before it even gets started. And even if they do stay engaged, if you say something like, "I feel angry about your bad attitude," it only sends a subjective message about how you feel. The point here isn't about how you feel; it's about the employee's bad attitude manifested in bad behavior and why it needs to change.

Equally ineffective is a statement like, "If you got your work done on time, we'd achieve this HARD goal and make my life a lot easier." This doesn't provide any objective facts that give the Talented Terror a reason to tune in to what you are saying. The employee may not dare say it aloud, at least not to your face, but he or she is probably thinking, "Who cares how you feel or what I can do for you. I've got more important things to do on company time, like posting to my blog and downloading music from iTunes."

However, if you keep the statement objective and say something like, "Company policy states your responsibility is to fulfill your work commitments on time. I just went into a meeting with Client X without the information I needed because I didn't have your work," you're putting the unemotional and objective facts on the table. And that presents a level of culpability that, even for the most calculating of Talented Terrors, is hard to slip out of.

Keeping a conversation about bad attitude objective presents a challenge that many leaders don't know how to meet. That's because there's a common, and incorrect, belief that objectivity is dependent upon being able to make a quantifiable analysis of a situation. In other words, you need to be able to measure it.

But just because you can't assign a number to attitude doesn't make it invalid. In fact, it's easy to lay an objective claim on the outward expression of attitude: behavior. A bad attitude nearly always leaks out in the form of bad behavior, and behavior absolutely can be verified and observed.

Southwest Airlines, the Ritz-Carlton, and Disney are all famous for their unique brands of customer service. And in all three organizations, that reputation is heavily dependent on employee attitude. These organizations are almost 100% able to assess whether or not employees have the right attitude. You don't catch Mickey Mouse grumbling about the heat any more than you find a Ritz-Carlton employee who's apathetic to a customer's needs. Nor are you likely to run into a "no-fun" Southwest flight attendant. In these companies, employee attitude is measured by behavior, and it's measured often. And when the behavior fails to match expectations, the employee is held accountable.

When you keep a conversation about bad attitude objective, the focus stays on the bad behavior. This prevents Talented Terrors from slipping through their favorite loophole, defensiveness, and turning the blame on you. All they can do is debate the options you present and decide whether or not it's personally worth it for them to continue with their bad attitude. That means any decisions they make will belong entirely to them, and that translates to long-term results.

Specificity

When tackling tough issues like attitude, it's critical to keep the conversation limited to specific events. Observable details about the bad behavior in question are what you're after, and you want those specifics at your fingertips. There's no need to inflate the specifics to make them severe enough to have a serious conversation. If you've seen unacceptable behavior, you're allowed, and in fact obligated, to address it.

Being specific also means avoiding absolutes in the form of words like "always" and "never." (Here's my rule: it is *always* a good idea to *never* use words like "always" and "never.") These words are nothing more than hyperbole. Absolutes only draw the emphasis away from the specifics and kill any chance you've got at keeping the focus on the facts. No one is always or never anything. Are you "always" on time or "never" wrong? Probably not, and neither are your Talented Terrors.

Accusing a Talented Terror of always showing up late and never being productive in meetings is laying the groundwork for failed communication. The employee is only going to battle off your accusation by dredging up the memory of some meeting that took place three years ago to which he or she not only arrived early, but also brought the doughnuts. Remember, these folks have been honing their bad-attitude skills for a long time. They're good at it, and they're smart, which means you have to be smarter.

Candor

There's no dodging the truth when you're talking to an employee about a bad attitude. It may seem kinder to surround a tough message in an attractive wrapper, but that won't get the facts out on the table, and it won't help to solve the problem. Fudging or inflating the truth doesn't do anybody any favors. You can't control how someone is going to react to your message, but you can control the message.

Don't make the common mistake of trying to squeeze a negative performance critique or correction between layers of positive reinforcement. Once again, it's called the Compliment Sandwich, and it doesn't work.

Imagine you're Frank, and your boss has just called you in for a little feedback. "Frank, you're a world-class programmer, the absolute best. You're probably the smartest guy in the department. You've been pretty nasty during our weekly meetings, and it's causing some hurt feelings. But I'm saying all this because you're just so darn talented, I want to see you really flourish."

What did you hear? If I'm Frank, I just heard: "I'm great; I'm smart." Waa waa waa waa. "I'm great; I'm smart."

Frank heard some compliments, then Charlie Brown's teacher, then some more compliments. But he certainly didn't hear anything about his job being in jeopardy or even his performance being anything other than great.

Not only is this message completely disingenuous, but as I said in Chapter 3, no one remembers what happens in the middle. Consider for a moment that you and two of your coworkers have each been given the opportunity to present a project before the board. Based upon the presentations, only one project will be chosen for funding. Are you going to want to speak first, second, or third? Most people opt for the third or first slot and do anything to avoid the dreaded middle position. Don't allow your message to become the ignored middle child. Get it out there in plain sight, because if your message isn't being heard, you aren't doing anything to resolve the problem.

If you're really afraid that blatant candor will shut down the conversation, you can always use a softening statement: one that won't mask your message. Try saying something like, "Frank, I've got a tough message to deliver. There's no getting around it, but I want you to understand that I'm doing this out of a concern for your well-being; because if you don't fix this stuff, your career here is in jeopardy." This softens the blow while enforcing the message: "You really need to listen to this." This is, by far, a blunt version of the IDEALS script (and if these people weren't such difficult Talented Terrors, that's the script you would use).

Calm

Staying calm may sound trivial or obvious, but Talented Terrors have a unique ability to get under a leader's skin. Chances are that when you call these folks in to discuss a bad attitude, you're going to have some emotion behind it; usually some form of anger or frustration. However, if you lose your cool, your argument is going to come off over the top and lose impact.

Remember, Talented Terrors have had plenty of time to hone their bad behavior, and they know how to wield it like a pro. They're used to getting called on their bad attitude, and they're just waiting for you to get angry and speak without thinking. Because as soon as you say or do something illogical, they'll turn the situation around on you. And before you know it, you'll end up apologizing to them for your bad behavior.

Remaining calm can be especially challenging for leaders who tend to jack up their anger as a means of getting and staying tough. Intimidators, for example, are more likely to uncork on a Talented Terror when their buttons get pushed (and when that happens, the Talented Terror has won). By contrast, Appeasers suffer the opposite problem and can become apologetic (which the Talented Terror interprets as weakness, which he or she uses to dominate the conversation).

But you don't have to be a victim of your own emotions. You can pay attention to what sets you off and respect it. When you see it coming your way, dodge the bullet. If you know you're easily led to anger when you're tired, don't even attempt to carry out a tough conversation after a poor night's sleep. If you get cranky when you're hungry, don't hold an important meeting before lunch.

The HALT approach is one that most 100% Leaders abide by. It's an easy and effective method of keeping anger and other unproductive emotions at bay. If you're hungry, angry, lonely, or tired (HALT), all of which are emotionally compromised positions, delay the conversation until your mood shifts or you can get some sleep or food. It's not like you're trying to step out on the discussion or avoid it; you're just rescheduling it.

Choice

Leadership grants you a certain level of authority, but you still can't force people to do something against their will. If you try and box Talented Terrors into a corner, their behavior will just get worse. They'll also become defensive and assume an attacking position that makes it impossible to reach the resolution you want. This only delivers results that are the complete opposite of your goal to eradicate the behaviors associated with the bad attitude.

All you can do is outline the choices and enforce the consequences. At that point, it's up to your Talented Terrors whether they decide to walk away, continue on with their bad behavior and face the outlined negative consequences, or change their behavior and enjoy the reward of positive consequences. But while the choice is up to them, you can still control how long they have to make that choice.

After you lay out the facts and outline the consequences, offer your Talented Terrors the option of taking 24 hours to think things over. You've likely given them a lot to take in, and they alone bear the burden of making a decision about how they will respond. By giving them some time to think it over, they're going to make a smarter decision; one they are more likely to abide by.

Script for Tying Together the Six Rules

By following the six rules, it's easy to construct a script that will address any attitudinal issue. Let's take a look at how it all comes together.

"Joe, I've called you in today because there's a problem with your recent performance. In Tuesday's task force meeting you made three biting and sarcastic remarks during our brainstorming session, and that's just not acceptable behavior for that setting. This will not be allowed to continue.

"Now, I can't force you to change, and I won't try. So you have a choice: you can change your behavior or keep it where it is. If you change, you will be much more effective, and I think you'll see your teammates respond more positively. If you decide to change, I can work with you to outline a very specific action plan with clear expectations. If you opt not to change, then we'll begin an improvement plan which, without significant progress, could ultimately result in termination. <Insert your own HR policies here.>

"Joe, I believe you are capable of changing this behavior. But only you can choose the path that's right for you. Just be clear that there are only two options here, and maintaining your present course is not one of them. You can give me your decision right now, or you can take 24 hours to make a decision."

How to Deal with the Response

After you deliver the script, there are a number of responses you might get. A perfect response would be acceptance. For instance, Joe would say, "You're absolutely correct, and I want to get back on track right away."

Typically, when you deliver the script correctly, it will go one of two ways. You're going to get either acceptance or the complete opposite, where the employee states an unwillingness to play by the rules and expresses a desire to just get out.

But sometimes you'll get a slightly different response such as:

Denial. "But I didn't do anything wrong."

Narcissism. "You can't come down on me; I'm the best person you've got!"

Anger. "How dare you insult me like this."

Blame. "Bob's the one you should be talking to; he's the one who always messes up."

Drama. This includes tears or other forms of histrionics.

Regardless of the response you get, there's a simple technique I told you about earlier, in Chapter 2, that will keep the conversation on track. It's what psychologists call the broken record technique, and it works just like it sounds: "I hear you; now let me repeat <insert script here>." And you walk the employee through the whole script again.

The broken record technique works as long as you stick to the script and don't indulge whatever defense the Talented Terror is offering up. These folks may be low performers, but they're not stupid. As I've said, they are often brilliant, and they are much better at having a bad attitude than you are at managing it. The only chance you have at keeping the communication on track, and not allowing yourself to be manipulated, is to stick to the script and the six rules. You may have to repeat the script two or three times, but after that it's time to say, "OK, I have made my point. This conversation is over."

Sticking to the script and keeping the conversation on track can feel a bit awkward at first. And Talented Terrors will try everything to get you off your script. Keep in mind that good management is by and large a performing art. And just like any performer, you need to practice. If you have teenagers, they typically love to play the role of Talented Terror, and they make wonderful practice partners. They'll give you every form of bad attitude and drama you can think of, and that will force you to get comfortable with calmly repeating yourself.

If They Agree to Make a Change

If a Talented Terror agrees to make a change for the better, you
need to be right on the ball with getting the person started toward
redemption. This includes explaining exactly what it will take to
meet expectations and how improvement will be measured. Providing Talented Terrors with a breakdown of what bad, good, and
excellent behavior looks and sounds like gives them a definitive
guide by which they can judge for themselves whether or not they
are on track.

Over the years, we've developed a technique called Word Pictures. It's a system for using your words to paint a picture of performance expectations. In essence, we describe three levels of
performance (Needs Work, Good Work, and Great Work) with
behaviorally specific language (i.e., you could clearly visualize how
each of the three categories would look). We do this for the following reasons:

> First, the three levels of performance allow employees to
> accurately rate their own performance. If someone only
> knows what Good Work looks like, it's hard to judge
> when a slip into poor performance takes place or when
> some extra effort produces desirable Hundred Percenter
> status. There's simply no way to evaluate your own
> performance if you don't specifically know what the boss
> considers bad, good, and great.
> Second, Word Pictures allow for consistency of performance
> expectations from manager to manager and from
> department to department. Too often an employee can be

viewed as a Hundred Percenter in one department only to be a middle or low performer, or even a Talented Terror, in another. It's often not that their performance has changed; it's just that different managers have different levels of expectations (you have to walk on water to be a middle performer in Department A, but you can sleepwalk and be a high performer in Department B).

I should note that if you develop Word Pictures for everyone in the organization and use them as part of your performance management system, you will avoid a great many performance problems (including Talented Terror issues). We've helped hundreds of organizations develop Word Pictures as part of their performance management process (not just for Talented Terrors), and in virtually every case, overall performance improves and incidents of Talented Terrors decrease significantly. Also diminished is the arguing about appraisal scores that typically takes place during every annual performance review.

The key to effective Word Pictures is explicit language. An easy way to gauge explicitness is to ask a complete stranger to the organization if he or she can follow what you're saying. Another test is to ask whether two different managers would give the same evaluation to one employee. If the answer is yes, you're on target. We have developed an entire library of Word Pictures to help our clients design performance appraisals and action plans. But let me share, in Table 5-1, a concrete example of a behavioral analysis one leader gave to an employee whose bad attitude was largely expressed through behaviors that showed a lack commitment to the job. The Needs Work category describes this Talented Terror to a tee.

Table 5-1. Word Pictures

Needs Work: I often arrive late to work and meetings or leave early. I avoid extra work, and when working in a team, I allow my coworkers to do most of the work. I am often found making personal calls and chatting at length with others about non-work-related topics. My attendance record is poor, with more than four days (as defined by the attendance policy) of unscheduled time off in any rolling six-month period. I display a lack of enthusiasm in my work. I appear overwhelmed by the demands of the organization's high-paced environment.

Good Work: I stay on task in spite of distractions and interruptions. I carry my own fair share of the workload. I don't wait to be told to take action and often look for an opportunity to help move a project along. I display an obvious sense of urgency. I carry out commitments displaying a high energy level. I respect the attendance policy and avoid missing work unnecessarily—usually only two or three unscheduled absences during the year. I accept personal responsibility for quality and timeliness of work without making excuses or blaming others.

Great Work: I display enthusiasm for each new project. I take pride in my work and am often asked to assume leadership positions. If I am unsure about something or uncover an unexpected problem, I take immediate action to remedy the situation and to bring it to the attention of others in order to avoid the problem in the future. I never miss work (no unscheduled absences), I never leave a site or job with unfinished business, and I see every project through to the end.

This goes a lot further than just saying, "I want you to be committed to the job." With Word Pictures, the employee can clearly see the Hundred Percenter attitudes you want and what the behaviors that accompany them look like. In the vast majority of cases, just like the one above, a bad attitude can be changed with just a 10-minute explanation.

Conclusion

Some leaders are leery about the simplicity of following a script based on the six rules. How can something this straightforward really work? Some leaders want to take a more aggressive approach; get in there and bop the Talented Terror upside the head until the employee cries uncle and submits to Hundred Percenter performance. Others feel a need to reach out to Talented Terrors and help them emotionally figure out where their bad attitude comes from. Neither of these methods works.

The six-rule technique is based on Leadership IQ's close observation of 100% Leaders who are managing Talented Terrors with success. We can confidently say that it works. It's a simple way to avoid the emotional roller-coaster ride these folks can take you on while clearly saying, "These are the rules on what's acceptable and what's not. If you follow the rules, you choose success. If not, you get removed."

Conclusion

$\mathbf{F}$ollowing my speeches that cover Hundred Percenters, I'm often asked if there any special secrets my trainers and I use when we implement these techniques with our clients. The answer is yes, but let me offer a caveat: each of our clients is a little different. For some organizations, we develop their employee survey; for others, we handle their leadership training; for some, we're doing 360° leadership assessments, or we might be designing their Hundred Percenter performance appraisal; and for others still, we revamp all their goals and goal-setting processes. And, of course, for some clients, we do everything.

Depending on the mix of assistance we're providing, my "implementation secrets" are going to vary. We've put lots of free downloadable resources on our Web site (www.leadershipiq.com), so I invite you to visit and get the answers you need to your very specific questions.

I've also distilled the Top 10 Lessons for creating a Hundred Percenter culture in your organization. These quick lessons will reinforce some of the key insights from the book and provide some specific steps with which to get started.

Lesson #1: Make Every Goal HARD

If you get no other lesson from this book, take away the idea that your goals need to be HARD. And that means everybody's goals. If you're the CEO, you can't ask your employees to achieve HARD goals if your goals aren't HARD. The same goes for trustees, vice presidents, managers, supervisors, and team leaders. The very first step I suggest you take is to review all your goals and see if they meet the HARD goal criteria outlined in Chapter 1. If not, rewrite them. And yes, you are allowed (and in fact obligated) to rewrite your goals throughout the year.

Lesson #2: Integrate HARD Goals into Performance Management

Once you've made sure that you've got HARD goals, take it one step further. Integrate those goals into every nook and cranny of your organization, including your performance management systems (e.g., performance appraisals). In Chapter 5, I showed you a technique called Word Pictures that we use to develop Hundred Percenter Performance Appraisals (you can learn even more about it on our Web site). Don't set HARD goals and then evaluate your folks using an entirely different set of criteria. If you want Hundred Percenters, evaluate, reward, and coach people using your HARD goals.

Lesson #3: Measure Whether You Have a Hundred Percenter Culture

Employee surveys, if they're well designed, can be great tools for telling you whether or not you have a Hundred Percenter culture (and what steps you need to take to get one). However, most surveys are terribly designed. So, first, read the Appendix, called "Why 5-Point Scales Don't Work (and Other Problems with Employee Surveys)." This will give you the techniques you need to design a great employee survey. Second, survey your employees (as long as it's been at least six months since your last survey, you're in the clear). If you asked your employees if they're "satisfied," but if you didn't ask if they're giving 100% or if their boss is pushing them to achieve greatness, then you probably didn't learn anything that's going to help you build a Hundred Percenter culture. Not only do you need some useful data, but there is simply no faster way to communicate your Hundred Percenter desires than by asking some great questions on an employee survey. (Remember, every question you ask communicates what you believe as a leader.)

Lesson #4: Measure Whether You Have 100% Leaders

In the Introduction, I mentioned some studies involving our 360° leadership assessments. I strongly recommend an assessment like this to evaluate the strengths and weaknesses of your leaders. Do you have 100% Leaders? Or do you have Appeasers, Intimidators, and Avoiders? Before you can create a road map that leads to a Hundred Percenter culture, you need to know exactly what kind of leaders you have driving the organization. Equally, these folks need to know what kind of leaders they are (otherwise, they'll never develop the critical self-awareness required to achieve significant change). Once you've evaluated your leaders, you're ready for the next lesson.

Lesson #5: Train Your Leaders to Be 100% Leaders

What's the first big step that an engineer takes on the road to becoming an engineer? Or a doctor? Or a lawyer? Or any other professional? The first step is training—lots and lots of training (high school, college, graduate school, professional education, whatever). And yet what's the first step in becoming a leader? It begins with a promotion (for technical ability, not leadership skills), followed by getting an office, then a budget binder, then a quick tutorial from HR on "how not to get sued," and finally a pat on the back. Oh, and let's not forget, we then completely abandon that person. Just count up the number of hours of formal and on-the-job training it takes to become a great professional. Then compare that number with the number of hours of training you give your leaders. Now, if you believe leadership is just common sense, then you should be paying your leaders way less than your frontline employees. Why are you making six, seven, or eight figures for a job that's just common sense? However, if you believe it takes training to become a 100% Leader (and that leaders are worth the money they get paid), then get started delivering some training right now. You can visit our Web site for some suggested training outlines.

Lesson #6: Learn Everyone's Shoves and Tugs

You've already learned that getting people motivated to become Hundred Percenters isn't that complicated (eliminate Shoves and implement Tugs). But this process does require discipline, courage, and some interpersonal intelligence. That's why even though the techniques are elegantly simple, so few leaders use them effectively. Just get started, give it a try, evaluate each of your conversations, and adjust as necessary. As you conduct your Shoves and Tugs conversations, track them organizationally. Within the first 60 days, you'll identify the key motivational drivers for your organization, and you'll know exactly which motivational levers to pull to create an entire culture of Hundred Percenters.

Lesson #7: Reach for Higher Stages of Accountability

Take the Stages of Accountability (Denial, Blame, Excuses, Anxiety, and Accountability), and do a quick estimate of what percentage of your employees lives in each stage. (A good employee survey, like the Hundred Percenter Index, will tell you this with great accuracy.) I can virtually guarantee that you don't have 100% in the Accountability Stage. So start to work on giving feedback, lots and lots of feedback. Watch a professional sports team, and look at how much feedback each player gets. An NFL player might get 100 to 200 pieces of feedback (big and small) throughout a 60-minute game. By contrast, a typical employee might get 2 pieces of feedback a week (and that could easily be 2 bits of feedback a month in many organizations). If you use the IDEALS script, you don't have to worry about people taking feedback the wrong way. Elite athletes need lots of real-time feedback. Hundred Percenter employees are no different.

Lesson #8: Turn Your Hundred Percenters into Heroes

Keep your Hundred Percenters energized, and use them as the models for teaching every other employee in your organization. At least once a week, you should be telling a quick story of a Hundred Percenter in a way that not only positively reinforces that individual, but also teaches others what they need to do. CEOs should bring a few frontline Hundred Percenters to the next board meeting. Vice presidents should bring a few to the next executive team meeting. Stop lamenting that there are no more great heroes. Find your Hundred Percenters, and put them on display.

Lesson #9: Improve or Remove Your Talented Terrors

Repeat after me: "There's no such thing as a high performer with a bad attitude." Go out on the front lines and ask your Hundred Percenters how much they enjoy working with Talented Terrors. I've yet to see a situation where Hundred Percenters prefer working with Talented Terrors over working short staffed. It's ironic, but one of the quickest ways to make a positive change to your organizational culture is to improve or remove your Talented Terrors. You'll feel like a weight has been lifted from your shoulders, and so will everyone else.

Lesson #10: Start Wherever You Can

Don't stand on ceremony—don't wait until every single person has bought in, and don't wait until you have the budget to address every single piece. Do something now. Pick an area of critical importance (revamping goals, training leaders, surveying employees, etc.), and get started. You don't need lots of fanfare. You just need leaders to read the book, to start discussing it, and then, bit by bit, to start challenging and connecting with their employees. Is it easier if the board and CEO "get it" and commit every single leader and employee to the Hundred Percenter cause? Sure it is. But sometimes that takes time to achieve. Remember what the great anthropologist Margaret Mead said, "Never doubt that a small group of thoughtful, committed people can change the world. Indeed, it is the only thing that ever has."

Appendix

Why 5-Point Scales Don't Work (and Other Problems with Employee Surveys)

I reference a lot of research throughout this book, much of which comes from employee surveys (and specifically our own survey tool called the Hundred Percenter Index). Employee surveys are powerful tools for understanding where you are on your 100% journey (including what level of Challenge and Connection your employees are currently experiencing). This is critical information to have when creating a road map that will lead to a Hundred Percenter workforce.

However, there is an element of danger to employee surveys— a danger of which many leaders remain unaware. Because employee surveys have such powerful potential, if they're designed or implemented incorrectly, their power can turn destructive. When this happens, it sends leaders and employees spiraling backward on the path to 100%.

In this section, I'm going to offer some of the best-practice discoveries my team of researchers and I have made over the past two decades about how to conduct employee surveys so they guarantee positive and useful results. And yes, we do use all these techniques in our own Hundred Percenter Index.

Discovery #1: 5-Point Scales Don't Work

In employee surveys (think of a Likert-type scale ranging from Strongly Disagree to Strongly Agree), 5-point scale types are what you most commonly find. In fact, these scales are so commonplace, and they've been around for so long, that I have even used them in our employee surveys (albeit many years ago). In many situations, 5-point scales are just fine, and psychological and sociological researchers use them to great effect. However, in the world of employee surveys, the 5-point scale has a fatal flaw.

Five-point scales were designed for situations where the data have a reasonable chance of being normally distributed—where there are decent odds that as many people will score 1s as they do 5s. If you asked 1,000 random people to rate the statement "Orange is a more fashionable color than green," you're going to get a wide variety of responses. Some people hate orange, while others love it. The same goes for green. And then there are the folks who feel so-so about both colors. You could ask people about any number of statements (e.g., "The Yankees are the best baseball team") and get a similarly wide spread of responses. In all these situations, a 5-point scale works just fine because the responses will be so varied.

But inside an organization, the 5-point scale loses its effectiveness. Inside organizations, 5-point survey results tend to be skewed and have less variability than results from the population at large. In other words, you won't get nearly as many 1s as 5s.

If you ask a group of employees at ACME Inc. to rate the statement "ACME is a good place to work," you're not going to get very many low responses (i.e., 1s and 2s). That's because if you truly thought ACME was an awful place to work, you probably would have quit already. By virtue of being an employee at ACME, you're saying, "Well, it can't really be all that bad because I keep showing up." (Of course, some employees truly dislike your organization, but not enough to give you a normal distribution of data.)

When you survey people who have said that the company is decent (judging by the fact that they show up every day), your survey results will be skewed toward Strongly Agree, and there won't be much variability in the responses. In the majority of the 5-point employee surveys we've seen, there really isn't a 5-point scale; it's more like a 3-point scale. Can you really say you're using a 1-to-5-point scale if all the responses come out 3, 4, or 5? (Test this yourself: make your survey company run a histogram of the responses on every single question, and see how badly skewed your data are. For you statistics nuts, you can also ask the company to calculate skewness and kurtosis.)

Nobody in his right mind is going to use a 3-point scale for an employee survey. It would essentially limit the choices to "Everything's Bad," "Everything's Great," or "It's So-So." And in the real world, things aren't quite so black and white. There's a notable difference between the grades A and B, or between an A and a B+, or even between an A and an A–. If you're comfortable grading your organization on pass-fail, which is kind of what you're doing when you get this very low spread of data, then go for it. But when an employee quits, it's probably not for an "Everything's Bad" reason—

like the manager is the devil incarnate, none of the computers work, and all my coworkers are low-performing losers. It's likely to be a bit more subtle than that; something the data results of a 5-point scale won't even begin to reveal.

If your employees aren't giving 100%, wouldn't you like to know just how far away they are from 100%? Do you really want to limit yourself to "It's 100% or nothing?" When I've held the position of CEO, I always wanted to know just how far away from 100% we really were. That's what told me how many resources to mobilize and what specific actions to take. There's a big difference between missing your sales targets by 1% and missing them by 50%. With a 5-point scale (which, in reality, becomes a 3-point scale), you'll never know which it is. You'll only know you missed your target.

This isn't the only bad news about 5-point scales. When you conduct employee surveys every year (or two), ceiling effects and restriction of range inhibit your ability to track your progress. Employee surveys frequently assess very subtle issues, and the interventions that follow often make numerically small, but very significant, changes. But if you're getting only three different responses, how do you see progress? Can you really assess your changes if your scale doesn't distinguish between decent, good, and great?

The easy resolution is a 7-point scale, which will accurately assess your employees. And for reasons of question design, I suggest making your scale range from Never to Always (instead of Strongly Disagree to Strongly Agree). Now, it's true that because you're assessing a biased pool of respondents, you will still see some skewing on a 7-point scale (you won't get lots of 1s and 2s). In fact, what you'll end up with is basically a 5-point scale.

To reiterate: if you start with a 5-point scale, you basically end up with a 3-point scale (because you lose the 1s and 2s). If you start with a 7-point scale, you basically end up with a 5-point scale (because, again, you lose the 1s and 2s). Here's the bottom line:

The respondent pool for employee surveys is positively biased. So when you give yourself a broader survey scale, your results more accurately capture the full range of true responses.

You may be tempted to ask, "If 7 points are better than 5, why not use a 10-point scale; it's even broader?" Ten-point scales have two significant flaws. First, there's no middle point on a 10-point scale. Just look at it; how do you give a score that is exactly equidistant between the highest and lowest scores (there's no 5.5 on your survey scale)? A properly designed survey scale needs a middle point.

The second problem is that 10-point scales often have more skewing than 7-point scales because we're mentally locked into a grade-based framework (from our years in school) where 10 is an A+, 9 is an A, 8 is a B, 7 is a C, and 6 and below are failing. Given our historical relationship with grades, survey respondents are often hesitant to give a score of 5 or below (because that's failing so badly that even our teachers in school were hesitant to use scores that low).

Our employee survey, the Hundred Percenter Index, uses a 7-point scale. And when we've taken over from other survey companies (many businesses change survey companies every few years), we've found significantly greater spread with our 7-point scale. It all adds up to much smarter decision making and far more accurate tracking of progress.

Discovery #2: Don't Ask Questions You Can't Fix

Here's the big lesson: Every survey question you ask implies a promise that you're going to do something positive with the answer you get. So if you don't know exactly what actions will fix a situation, don't ask a question about it until you do. Otherwise, you're setting the stage for employees to doubt your leadership capabilities: "Gee, the boss asked how we felt about X, we all said lousy, and then he did nothing about it."

Surveys commonly ask questions about whether employees have friends at work and whether they trust their boss. Let's say you get low scores on those questions. Obviously, now you need to do something about it. Let's start with the trust issue. Do you know specifically what causes the typical employee to trust the boss? How about what specifically causes your unique employees to trust the boss? And what steps have you taken to validate these issues?

We conducted one of the largest studies ever on just this topic: what makes employees trust their boss (*hint:* it's *not* being honest and truthful). We discovered that the extent to which leaders respond constructively to employees who bring them work-related problems is the biggest driver of employee trust. This factor ranked significantly higher than whether or not the employees saw the boss as honest and truthful. And yet there are a lot of organizations teaching managers to engender greater trust by being more honest, while other organizations are teaching managers to be more transparent in order to gain employee trust. What is the guaranteed solution to the problem? You won't find an answer by asking a question like, "Do you trust your boss?"

Similarly, low scores on a question that asks if employees have a good friend at work don't teach you exactly what steps you need to take to fix the issue. Social networking *might* improve friendships, but so might more teamwork or less teamwork, or spending more time together or less time together, etc. The solution might depend on your unique culture. Bottom line, if you really want to know what's going to work for your folks, you've got to ask about those solutions specifically.

It should also be noted that factors like friendships and trust are means to an end; they are not the end themselves. The end is to get employees to willingly and passionately give 100% and to recruit people to come to the company and do the same. Maybe having friends at work is causally related to that; maybe it's not. Maybe trust is causally related to that; maybe it's not. Maybe having open communication, doing interesting work, having good life balance, being autonomous, or being in great teams are all related, but maybe they're not. The trick is to figure out what's truly related and ask about it in a way that gives you information about the specific actions you need to take.

On the Hundred Percenter Index, every question asked includes a clear path of action. So if you discover an area you need to fix, you'll immediately know what needs to be done. We'll never ask employees if they trust their boss. However, we will ask if the boss responds constructively when presented with work-related problems. We'll also never ask employees if they have a good friend at work. However, we will ask if the employees can successfully deliver constructive feedback to their coworkers.

The Hundred Percenter Index has the solutions built right in, but the same cannot be said of most employee survey questions. To judge how effective your current employee survey really is, take a good look at every question on the survey, and ask yourself, "Do I know exactly what actions will fix this issue?" It's not good enough to be able to guess what might work; you have to know with complete certainty what you will do. If you don't have a definitive answer, the survey question has no value and needs to be dropped.

Discovery #3: Train Your Managers How to Take Action

As a follow-up to Discovery #2, it's important to conduct employee surveys only if you're prepared to give your managers the specific tools needed to correct the issues identified. My research has found it takes a minimum of two solid days of training to equip managers with enough skills to do the job effectively.

If your survey discovers that employees find performance feedback is weak, you need to teach managers how to deliver robust feedback. If your survey discovers that employees don't fully understand the goals set by their manager, you need to teach managers how to clearly set and communicate goals. If your survey discovers that employees don't think their manager holds low performers accountable, you need to teach managers how to hold low performers accountable. And so on.

I've seen more organizations than I care to count that conduct surveys without giving their managers all the specific skills and tools they need to implement the changes. The result is frustrated managers and irritated employees. The reality is that if managers were ready to make all the necessary changes without any further training, they would have done it already. Giving your managers employee survey data without the right management training is the equivalent of sending someone to work in the ER of a hospital without medical training. (And that's why I won't take on a new survey client unless the client is prepared to give managers some training following the survey.)

Discovery #4: 10 Questions Are Not Enough

It doesn't matter whether you ask 9 questions on your survey or 10 or 12 or 14 questions. None of these numbers is likely to be big enough to help you figure out exactly what makes your unique group of employees tick.

I've run hundreds of regression analyses from similarly sized organizations that show that one group of employees is usually driven by radically different issues than another. For instance, a nurse in a small community hospital in Alabama is likely to have different motivational drivers than a stock trader on Wall Street, or a government employee, or a soldier in Iraq, or a Gen Y programmer in Silicon Valley—just as a commissioned salesperson will have different motivational drivers than a civil service employee. Each of these folks made radically different career choices, and they all have radically different work schedules, workloads, compensation packages, missions, levels of job risk, etc. So while some of these folks might do their job just fine without a best friend sitting next to them, others might be more motivated by taking on risky projects and still others by having greater security and predictability.

It takes 25 to 30 questions to really figure out what motivates your unique group of employees. Sure, it's fun and easy and relatively quick to ask just 12 questions (and you might save five minutes on your survey). But who cares if it's fast if the data you get completely miss the mark on the issues you need to know about? If you go to the doctor and she takes an extra five minutes to do a really thorough examination, are you going to be annoyed? Probably not. I mean, you took the time to drive there and get undressed; you might as well take a little extra time to get a medically accurate diagnosis. It's no different with employee surveys.

Discovery #5: Don't Aim for Mediocrity

Throughout this book, I've made the case that the key to success is tapping the unrealized Hundred Percenter potential of your employees. By pushing people beyond their self-imposed limitations, you can help them achieve truly great results and a depth of fulfillment previously unknown. And yet almost every employee survey in the world asks about some version of the statement "Overall, I am satisfied with company ABC." The only thing that will remain untapped in the question is the information you need, but won't get.

Let's imagine you score a perfect 7 out of 7 on this question (or even 5 out of 5 on your current survey). What does that really tell you? It says, "Absolutely, I am satisfied." It does *not* say, "I will drip blood, sweat, and tears to achieve this extraordinary goal in order to feel the addictive swell of pride and achievement." It can't say that, because you only asked if people felt satisfied. And being satisfied is a mediocre feeling when compared with the life-altering fulfillment that comes from giving 100%.

If I take my wife out for dinner and the manager comes by to ask if I'm satisfied, I could easily say yes and still never return to that restaurant. We have young kids, and our dinners out don't happen three nights a week (we'll get there again, but not right now), and so we try to make our dates really special. I'll be satisfied if the food and service are good, but if I have only two dates with my wife next month, I want our dinner to be more than satisfactory—I want it to be extraordinary. That's my expectation. But the restaurant manager didn't ask me if dinner was extraordinary; he only asked if it was satisfactory. I said yes because my food was delivered accurately and efficiently, but that doesn't tell the manager I won't be coming back again, or why. He only knows his staff didn't mess things up so horribly that I might ask for a refund. If he had asked me if I was blown away, he'd have gotten a very different answer, one that would actually give him valuable feedback.

When you ask employees if they're satisfied, you're only asking whether things are so messed up that they might go running for the exits. You still have no idea if they might leave you for a different company that's aiming for greatness. All you know is that things aren't awful; your employees are satisfied. If you want to know if they are deeply fulfilled and committed to giving 100% to achieve your goals, you have to ask.

This book is about how to take your employees from ordinary to extraordinary. Asking survey questions that inquire whether you're 100% maxed out on making folks ordinary doesn't serve that purpose. Why not ask your people how you're doing on making them extraordinary? (Visit www.leadershipiq.com to see some of the Hundred Percenter questions we recommend asking.)

Discovery #6: You've Got 28 Days

The results of your employee survey have an expiration date, and it's about 28 days from the ending of data collection. Too many companies complete the data collection piece and then wait three, four, or even five months to get their data back. That's simply too long. Employees took time out to sit down and give you some honest feedback, and they expect to know the results. When we sit on their responses for months on end, we may as well be saying, "Thanks for participating. Now we're going to do whatever we're going to do, and if we ever feel like telling you what that is, you'll be toward the bottom of the list of the people we tell." (That doesn't do anything for the morale you were trying to improve via the employee survey.)

When you ask people to exert effort to take the survey, the least you can do is honor that effort and give them back some data. You don't have to have every single regression run and every departmental data set completed, but you must let folks know that the initial report and analysis have been received and that there's a schedule for meetings where every employee can see or hear the results. If you wait three, four, or five months to do this, people will either get irritated or forget they even participated in taking the survey. And if they forget, they will have chalked it up to another one of the failed flavor-of-the-month initiatives the organization always tries, and your leaders' credibility will be seriously hurt.

If you conduct an employee survey, spend as much (or more) effort on distributing and acting on the data as you did on collecting the data. And by the way, don't ever let your survey provider tell you it takes months to process the data; it doesn't (unless you're at the bottom of the providers' priority list).

Index

About the Author

Mark Murphy is the founder and CEO of Leadership IQ. Since its inception, Leadership IQ has become a top-rated provider of leadership training, employee surveys, and e-learning. As the force behind some of the largest leadership studies ever conducted, Leadership IQ's live and online training programs have yielded remarkable results for such organizations as Microsoft, IBM, MasterCard, Merck, AstraZeneca, MD Anderson Cancer Center, FirstEnergy, Volkswagen, and Johns Hopkins. Murphy's cutting-edge leadership techniques and research have been featured in *Fortune, Forbes, BusinessWeek, U.S. News & World Report,* the *Washington Post,* and hundreds more periodicals. He was featured on a CBS News *Sunday Morning* special report on slackers in the workplace as well as being featured on ABC's *20/20.* He has also made several appearances on *Fox Business News.*

A former turnaround advisor, Murphy guided more than 100 organizations from precarious financial situations to record-setting levels of prosperity. For these and other accomplishments, Murphy was a three-time nominee for Modern Healthcare's Most Powerful People in Healthcare Award, joining a list of 300 luminaries including George W. Bush and Hillary Clinton. Only 15 consultants had ever been nominated to this list. He was also awarded the Healthcare Financial Management Association's Helen Yerger Award for Best Research.

A seasoned public speaker, Murphy has illuminated audiences for hundreds of groups and lectured at the Harvard Business School, Yale University, the University of Rochester, and the University of Florida.

For free downloadable resources, including quizzes and discussion guides, please visit www.leadershipiq.com.